Department for Culture, Media and Sport

Annual Report 2007

**Department for Culture,
Media and Sport –
Departmental Annual Report 2007**

Presented to Parliament by the Secretary
of State for Culture, Media and Sport and
the Chief Secretary to the Treasury by
Command of Her Majesty, May 2007.

Cm 7104   £18.00

Contents

About DCMS – the Department for Culture, Media and Sport

Our aim

DCMS aims to improve the quality of life for all through cultural and sporting activities, to support the pursuit of excellence and to champion the tourism, creative and leisure industries.

Our responsibilities

Our responsibilities include the arts, sport, the National Lottery, tourism, libraries, museums and galleries, broadcasting, press freedom and regulation, licensing and gambling and the creative industries from film to the music industry.

We are also responsible for the export licensing of cultural goods, the management of the Government Art Collection, the Royal Parks Agency and the historic environment, including the listing of historic buildings and scheduling of ancient monuments.

As part of our commitment to sport, we are responsible for the 2012 Olympic Games and Paralympic Games.

We also manage humanitarian assistance in the event of a disaster, such as the London bombings, as well as the organisation of the annual Remembrance Day Ceremony at the Cenotaph.

In 2006, we took legislation through Parliament to reform the National Lottery and set up the Big Lottery Fund, which replaced three earlier grant-giving bodies.

We share responsibility for Ofcom (a public corporation) and the Design Council (an executive NDPB), with the Department of Trade and Industry (DTI). Our functions are delivered through our three public corporations, two public broadcasting authorities, one executive agency (the Royal Parks Agency) and 57 non-departmental public bodies (NDPBs).

Our objectives

Our strategic objectives are to:

Children and young people
Further enhance access to culture and sport for children and give them the opportunity to develop their talents to the full and enjoy the benefits of participation.

Communities
Increase and broaden the impact of culture and sport, to enrich individual lives, strengthen communities and improve the places where people live, now and for future generations.

Economy
Maximise the contribution that the tourism, creative and leisure industries can make to the economy.

Delivery
Modernise delivery by ensuring our sponsored bodies are efficient and work with others to meet the cultural and sporting needs of individuals and communities.

Olympics
Host an inspirational, safe and inclusive Olympic Games and Paralympic Games and leave a sustainable legacy for London and the UK.

Foreword

This year's Annual Report has a new format. It uses the words of people around the country to illustrate some of the changes in our society that DCMS has helped to bring about. It covers a busy year with some significant landmarks.

The BBC gained a Royal Charter and will soon have a new licence fee. Work to get the country ready to switch to digital TV is on track. And getting London ready for the 2012 London Games and Paralympic Games has moved ahead at an impressive rate.

We believe that the 2012 Olympics will be the greatest show on earth. The budget is now settled; we're way ahead of where Athens or Sydney were when they were planning their Olympics, as work has already started on the London site; we are developing a Cultural Olympiad – a four-year celebration of the UK's cultural life; and are taking full advantage of the opportunity to boost the UK economy by transforming one of the most deprived parts of the country – the Lower Lea Valley, in East London.

After 2012, London and the UK will never be the same again. The Olympics will leave an impressive legacy of regeneration. They will create new facilities, a new city and a new national mood of optimism and excitement about sport, culture, our environment and design.

Success in the arts continues to thrive – as culture and creativity are at the heart of our lives in the UK. Record numbers of the public are attending exhibitions and British artists and performers are winning awards and acclaim all over the world. This is supported by the Prime Minister, Tony Blair, who heralded a 'golden age' in the arts and creative industries. High expectations, and the knowledge that the UK can become – and remain – the world hub for culture and creativity are the rationale behind our continuing case for public investment to keep us there.

Since 1997, the UK's cultural life and creative industries have been transformed. Record investment from the Government and soaring private sector support have reaped a high dividend that has touched the lives of a large proportion of the UK population. The arts impact in many key areas of Government policy including education, regeneration, youth engagement and tackling social exclusion.

I want to thank all the staff at DCMS and our colleagues at our partner organisations. This includes the ministerial team – Richard Caborn, David Lammy and Shaun Woodward. I would also like to welcome our new Permanent Secretary Jonathan Stephens, who joins us from the Treasury. He has already settled into his post admirably and is destined to be a huge asset to the Department.

Tessa Jowell.

Rt Hon Tessa Jowell MP
Secretary of State for Culture,
Media and Sport, and Minister
for the Olympics

Foreword

This is the Department's first Annual Report to Parliament since I was appointed Permanent Secretary. Most of this year's achievements were secured under the leadership of my predecessor, Dame Sue Street, who led the Department so effectively from 2001 to 2006.

In my first five months in DCMS I have been impressed by the enormous scope of this relatively small Department. In my first month alone I visited the Olympic site for the first time, viewed the collections at the V&A and Tate and stared into the football sized eye of a giant squid at the Natural History Museum.

Alongside this extraordinary diversity, DCMS has continued to deliver over the last year. Work on the Olympics has progressed apace, with the development of the Olympic Park remaining on schedule and £200 million funding allocated by the Treasury to support our elite athletes in their preparation for the Games. We delivered a new Charter for the BBC, which will make it stronger and more independent, and agreed the new Licence Fee settlement. We exceeded our PSA target of 75 per cent of school children spending a minimum of two hours a week on sport, and we launched a major review of how we protect our national heritage with the publication of the Heritage White Paper.

More will be expected of us in the future and I am committed to ensuring that the Department fulfils its potential. The Department's first Capability Review provided a great opportunity to focus on how we do this. I want DCMS to be clear about the value we add to our sectors and be driven by clear, consistent priorities. We should capitalise on our size by ensuring that it allows us to act quickly and be agile in reallocating resources, and we need to develop a more integrated and strategic approach to working with our sponsored bodies.

The Capability Review Team recognised the great talent, motivation and potential of our staff. Our successes are down to their commitment and contribution, working alongside our Ministerial team.

Jonathan Stephens

Jonathan Stephens
Permanent Secretary

The year's highlights

'The roadshow was brilliant. I can't wait for 2012!'

Community engagement

A focal point of the year was the first anniversary on 6 July 2006 of London's winning bid and the launch of the 'Be Part of 2012' roadshow. Organised in partnership with the London Organising Committee for the Olympic Games and Paralympic Games, the 22-day roadshow travelled over 5,000 kilometres across the UK, visiting every English region and Scotland, Wales and Northern Ireland, highlighting the benefits the Games will bring to many communities.

The roadshow started in Trafalgar Square, where thousands had cheered London's success a year before. It finished with an impressive firework display in Liverpool on 27 July 2006, six years to the day of the Opening Ceremony.

Enthusiasm and public support were confirmed with a UK-wide survey in December 2006 showing that 79 per cent of the population support the Games taking place in London in 2012 – higher than at any point since winning the bid.

Lizzie
Age 21

Visitor to the
'Be Part of 2012'
roadshow, Leeds

All milestones met

In April 2006 London hosted the first full visit of the International Olympic Committee's Co-ordination Commission. The Co-ordination Commission team visited a number of Games venues and received detailed reports on progress across a range of areas, from transport to culture. They warmly praised London's progress and our success in delivering all key milestones since winning the bid to host the 2012 Games.

At the end of the visit, Denis Oswald, Chair of the Co-ordination Commission, commended London's "ambitious and visionary project", recognising the "energy and excitement that this project is bringing to the city and the country".

In April, the Olympic Board also agreed its shared vision and objectives for the Games – to host an inspirational, safe and inclusive Games and to leave a sustainable legacy for London and the UK. In March 2007 the Secretary of State announced the final budget for the Olympic Delivery Agency, the body with responsibility for building venues for 2012 and delivering wider infrastructure improvements.

Olympic Park on schedule

The first major project began on site in April 2006. This is crucial to the overall regeneration of the area. Two tunnels are being constructed to take the 13 kilometres of powerlines that currently cross the Lower Lea Valley on 52 pylons. In April 2007 the first tunnel was completed on schedule and all tunnelling work is on track to be completed by summer 2007.

By December 2006, 93 per cent of the land needed for the Olympic Park had been secured and demolition work was underway. A new sports centre will be built to provide a training area during the Olympic Games. This will also host tennis and archery during the Paralympic Games and will benefit the local community after the Games.

The final Olympic Park Masterplan was agreed in June 2006. At the beginning of February 2007, the planning application for the Olympic Park was submitted. At 10,000 pages and 15 volumes, it is one of the largest ever applications in Europe and demonstrates the scale of our vision for the site. Meanwhile, work continued on the main sporting venues. Iconic designs were agreed for the Aquatics Centre and procurement began for the centrepiece Olympic Stadium and the Velopark (the cycling stadium).

Sustainable development remains integral to the development of the Park as well as the Games overall. Within the Park, this means that we will ensure that the biodiversity is enhanced, reviving the extensive waterways and restoring the plant habitats, whilst ensuring that it is accessible to all and that all elements of local communities are engaged in developing and using the Park and facilities. The Olympic Delivery Authority's Sustainable Development Strategy was approved by the Olympic Board and launched by the Prime Minister in January. It sets ambitious targets for low carbon emission, low waste and sustainable transport during the construction of Games venues and infrastructure. The Commission for a Sustainable London 2012 has been set up by the Olympic Board to report independently on sustainability for the overall programme.

Top: The first underground powerlines tunnel completed on the Olympic Park site earlier this year.

Above: The agreed design for the London 2012 Aquatics Centre which will host the swimming, diving and synchronised swimming events.

Paralympic hopes

Wheelchair rugby is Britain's fastest growing Paralympic sport, GB Team ranked fourth in the 2006 world championships.

Wheelchair rugby team The Bulls were voted the North East's favourite Lottery-funded project and made it to the UK final of The National Lottery Awards 2006.

Name: James
Location: UK League play-offs

'When I became paralysed I thought life was over, wheelchair rugby has given me a new lease of life, and one I thoroughly enjoy!'

'My ambition is to be a pro dancer. If you like something – do it!'

Ballet Changed My Life: Ballet Hoo!

The most high profile of the DCMS Cultural Pathfinder initiatives was the 'Leaps and Bounds' project which set out to show that the power of the arts, combined with effective partnership working, can transform lives. The project was filmed and in September 2006 the resulting documentary, *Ballet Changed My Life: Ballet Hoo!* (conceived by Neil Wragg of Youth at Risk, and Roy Ackerman of Diverse Productions), was broadcast on Channel 4.

The project took 200 young people in Birmingham, identified by local youth workers as 'at risk', and provided them with life coaches, a fitness regime and introduced them to the basic principles of ballet. Just under 100 participants enrolled for the much more intensive second stage which involved training at the Birmingham Royal Ballet for six months. It culminated on 28 September 2006 in a live performance of *Romeo and Juliet* at the Birmingham Hippodrome. The show achieved ratings of over one million people per episode. One of the participants summed up the profound effect of the experience: "I used to be a nobody – now I'm a somebody".

Ballet Hoo! received £100,000 funding from Arts Council England and £300,000 from local authorities. The project was designed and delivered by a partnership including the Birmingham Royal Ballet, Youth at Risk, Birmingham City Council, and Dudley, Wolverhampton and Sandwell Borough Councils. It was supported by the Learning and Skills Council and Black Country Connexions.

Jovan
Age 17

Participant of
Ballet Hoo!
Birmingham

Heritage Protection White Paper

After extensive consultation across the heritage sector, we published a White Paper on Heritage Protection Reform in March 2007. This sets out our proposals for a new heritage protection system that is simpler, more open to the general public and more flexible. It will enable our historic assets to be better understood and managed, whilst still continuing to protect them. It offers an opportunity to address a range of issues, including: the burden of the current heritage protection consent regimes and the scope for management agreements to reduce this; and the protection of archaeological sites on agricultural land and in the marine environment. There are five main strands to the White Paper:

- a unified Register of Historic Sites and Buildings of England that will bring together buildings, archaeology, parks, gardens, battlefields and World Heritage sites into a single system;

- a unified heritage consent regime that brings together Listed Building Consent and Scheduled Monument Consent;

- the use of statutory Heritage Partnership Agreements for owners of large, more complex sites;

- better guidance and support for local authorities, and some new powers to encourage Local Planning Authorities to give greater priority to heritage at local level; and

- an effective UK-wide marine heritage protection system, which provides appropriate protection for assets, is simple and clear and delivers designation decisions quickly.

Top: *The Sultan's Elephant* roaming through Hyde Park in May 2006.

Above: The Government Art Collection is a unique British cultural resource which displays works of art in British Government buildings both in the UK and around the world.

The collection includes Samuel Joseph's marble bust of William Wilberforce. This is a study for Joseph's monumental statue of Wilberforce in Westminster Abbey, which was installed in 1840 and is based on Jean-Antoine Houdon's portrait of Voltaire of 1781.

The Sultan's Elephant

For three days in May 2006, *The Sultan's Elephant* entertained Londoners and the city's visitors. A majestic 42-tonne, 12m high time-travelling mechanical elephant and a 5m 'little' girl giant roamed the streets in the biggest piece of free theatre ever seen in London. Over one million people came to see the event, which was created by the French theatre company Royal de Luxe and produced by Artichoke Productions. Bringing this breathtaking street theatre to London was also a logistical triumph requiring the collaboration of a network of funding and operational partners, including Arts Council England (ACE) and the Royal Parks. BBC4 brought this unique and enchanting event to an audience outside London with the documentary, *The Elephant and the Sultan*.

The Sultan's Elephant is a wonderful example of how the investment DCMS makes through ACE supports the arts.

Fifth anniversary of free entry to national museums and galleries

Government investment and changes to the tax laws have meant that well-known museums like the Natural History Museum and the V&A in London, the National Railway Museum in York and National Museums Liverpool have seen admissions soar by 29 million since 2001.

2006 was the best year for admissions to museums nationally since 2001. This represents an 83 per cent increase in total visits to museums that used to charge an entrance fee, an extra 6.5 million people. The *Renaissance in the Regions* programme of support for regional museums also surpassed its key participation targets. Over the last two years Hub museums attracted nearly two million new users, with over 900,000 of them coming from 'priority' groups. The number of visits by children aged 5-16 rose by 50 per cent in the three years to March 2006 – double what museums had been asked to achieve.

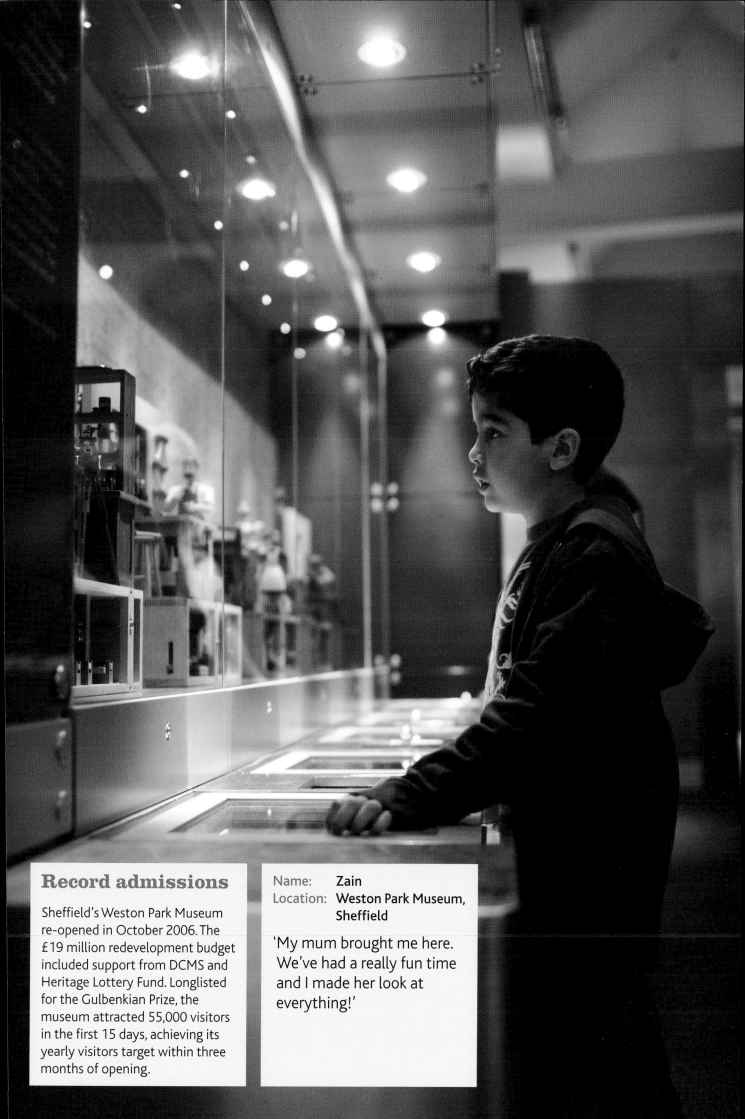

Record admissions

Sheffield's Weston Park Museum re-opened in October 2006. The £19 million redevelopment budget included support from DCMS and Heritage Lottery Fund. Longlisted for the Gulbenkian Prize, the museum attracted 55,000 visitors in the first 15 days, achieving its yearly visitors target within three months of opening.

Name: **Zain**
Location: **Weston Park Museum, Sheffield**

'My mum brought me here. We've had a really fun time and I made her look at everything!'

'Helping Mrs Nuttall with her new digital box meant so much to her'

Digital switchover

The only way we can achieve universal access to free-to-view terrestrial digital TV via an aerial is by switching off the analogue network and moving to digital-only terrestrial television broadcasting. In response to this, in September 2005, the Government confirmed that digital switchover will occur between 2008 and 2012. This will take place, ITV region by region, starting in the Border region. The Cumbrian town of Whitehaven will be a flagship project and will switch in October 2007.

The UK is making great progress in its goal to go digital. More than three-quarters of UK households are already enjoying the wider choice, sound and picture quality of digital TV.

2006 marked an important step towards switchover. In Bolton, we and the BBC managed a trial of the Digital Switchover Help Scheme, which will help the vulnerable to make the switch. Animated robot character 'Digit Al' also hit our television screens as the focal point for raising awareness. This major communications campaign is run by Digital UK, the independent, non-profit organisation leading the process of digital TV switchover.

Geoff
Age 63

RNIB volunteer
for the Digital
Switchover Help
Scheme, Bolton

A stronger independent BBC

The end of 2006 saw the expiry of the old BBC Charter and the introduction of a new Charter on the governance of the BBC over the next ten years. Following the most comprehensive consultation ever about a BBC Charter, the new Charter was sealed on 19 September 2006. It saw the replacement of the BBC Board of Governors with two new bodies: the BBC Trust and the Executive Board. The BBC Trust will oversee the Executive Board and will be the licence fee payer's voice, acting as proxy for the BBC's shareholders. It is the first public interest body on this scale in the UK. In April 2007 Sir Michael Lyons was appointed as the first chairman of the BBC Trust. The Trust will also have responsibility to ensure that the BBC's activities are not anti-competitive and are consistent with a vibrant and dynamic broadcasting market.

In creating the new Charter we have also defined the BBC's role and scope more clearly than before through a new set of six public purposes: sustaining citizenship and civil society; promoting education and learning; stimulating creativity and cultural excellence; reflecting the UK's nations, regions and communities; bringing the world to the UK and the UK to the world; and building a digital Britain. The new arrangements took full effect on 1 January 2007.

A new six-year licence fee settlement was announced on 18 January 2007. The settlement provides for annual nominal increases in the licence fee of 3 per cent for the first two years, and 2 per cent in years three, four and five. This means the price of a colour TV licence will rise from its current level of £131.50 to a figure of up to £151.50 in 2012. The settlement followed the most open process for setting the level of the licence fee ever, which took into account the views of the public and the industry, as well as independent advice and research.

Above: The BBC Trust works on behalf of licence fee payers: it ensures the BBC provides high quality output and good value for all UK citizens and it protects the independence of the BBC.

Get set for digital

From digital switchover to broadband and the People's Network, libraries have helped people learn about new technology and develop digital skills.

Since opening in March 2005 the Jubilee Library in Brighton has run sessions to actively support digital inclusion.

Name: Eileen
Location: Jubilee Library, Brighton

'I've learned so much about what you can do with all this digital technology.'

'Getting the funding has made everything so much easier'

UK Sport Olympic and Paralympic athlete funding package

Hosting an excellent Olympic and Paralympic Games in 2012 is not simply about building superb stadiums and athlete facilities. It is also about sending the largest, most talented Team GB to compete and win more medals than we have achieved in recent history.

Successful athletes need raw talent, dedication and commitment, with the best support teams around them, including coaches, sport scientists, and state of the art facilities. To win medals, we need the best high performance sport system in the world, for 2012 and beyond.

In March 2006, the Chancellor announced an additional £200 million Exchequer funding for Olympic and Paralympic athletes in advance of London 2012. He also called on the private sector to contribute £100 million to high performance sport. In summer 2006, UK Sport announced an additional £65 million for Olympic and Paralympic sport in the run up to the Beijing Games in 2008, taking the total investment to £215 million. Subject to a complete review of performance of all sports after Beijing, UK Sport has available £400 million to invest in high performance sport between the Beijing and London Games.

In addition UK Sport is investing £17 million from 2004-08 through the Talented Athlete Scholarship Scheme (TASS) and TASS 2012 to assist in the identification and nurturing of rising talent. 2,800 individual athletes have been supported through TASS in the first three years.

Eniola
Age 20

Talented Athlete Scholarship Scheme recipient, London

School sport

The National School Sport Strategy – being implemented jointly by the Department for Education and Skills (DfES) and DCMS – went live on 1 April 2003. DfES and DCMS share an ambitious PSA target to increase the percentage of 5-16 year olds spending at least two hours each week on high quality physical education (PE) and school sport, to 75 per cent by 2006 and 85 per cent by 2008. By 2010, the ambition is to offer all children at least four hours of sport a week. Over £1.5 billion (including Lottery funding) is being invested in PE and school sport from 2003 to 2008.

The 2005-06 PE, School Sport and Club Links survey found that:

■ 80 per cent of pupils in partnership schools participate in at least two hours of high quality PE and school sport in a typical week, exceeding the 2006 target by five percentage points. This represents an increase of almost 16 per cent on 2004-05 and 29 per cent on 2003-04;

■ in partnership schools during the 2005-06 academic year, 71 per cent of pupils were involved in intra-school competitive activities;

■ across Years 2-11, 27 per cent of pupils in partnership schools participated in at least one sports club linked to their school (this includes dance and multi-skill clubs). This represents a 22 per cent rise on 2004-05 and 42 per cent on 2003-04. The most common sports for which there were club links were football (78 per cent), cricket (52 per cent), rugby union (46 per cent), dance (40 per cent) and athletics (38 per cent);

■ across Years 10-13, 13 per cent of pupils in partnership schools have been actively involved in sports volunteering and leadership during the academic year. This represents an 18 per cent rise on 2004-05 and a 44 per cent rise on 2003-04.

The sporting landscape

The organisation of sport underwent a major reform on 1 April 2006, as had been announced by the Secretary of State in September 2005. This sought to streamline and clarify the respective roles and responsibilities of Sport England and UK Sport.

Sport England's focus was tightened to give them lead responsibility for increasing participation in sport at a community level, with responsibility for the English Institute of Sport, the successful Talented Athlete Scholarship Scheme (TASS), and the English elements of the UK 'performance pathway' – taking the athlete from talent identification through to the podium – being transferred to UK Sport.

The Secretary of State said: "Winning the Olympic Games was a huge achievement for sport in this country. It is vital that we capitalise on this once-in-a-generation opportunity to boost our medal hopes and drive up participation in sport. The changes will create a clear organisational distinction between community and elite sport."

An element of Lottery and Exchequer funding was transferred from Sport England to UK Sport in respect of these changes.

Top: Young leaders at the Step into Sport Camp, at Loughborough University.

Above: *The Active People* survey results, published in December 2006, show that 21 per cent of people (aged 16 plus) are taking part in 30 minutes of sport three times a week.

Breathing spaces

Millions of Londoners and tourists visit the eight Royal Parks for free each year. The 5,000 acres of historic parkland provide unparalleled opportunities for enjoyment, exploration and healthy living in the heart of the capital. The Hub in The Regent's Park offers a host of facilities for community and sporting activities.

Name: Kalli
Location: The Hub, The Regent's Park, London

'I run round here all the time. It's great to have such a lovely green space right in the centre of London.'

'The difference in all the bars round here is amazing. They're busier, but safer'

Licensing laws

On 24 November 2006, we celebrated the first anniversary of the new licensing laws. While firm conclusions about the impact of the new regime will not be drawn until the autumn of 2007, there is a broad consensus that there has not been the surge in crime and disorder predicted by some.

Emerging evidence already suggests the new licensing laws are helping local authorities and the police to manage the night-time economy better. For example, in the Broad Street area of Birmingham, strong partnership working and effective licence conditions have delivered real results. Broad Street now has a greater diversity of premises attracting customers in a wider age range and reported violent crime is down by over 50 per cent.

Consumer surveys in Birmingham indicate that:

■ 66 per cent of visitors regularly visit pubs, bars and clubs, up from 63 per cent in 2005; and

■ 49 per cent feel getting home is quicker and easier due to the provision of taxi marshals and extended licensing hours.

Iain
Age 43

Bar manager in
Broad Street,
Birmingham

Tourism Industry Emergency Response group

Intensive DCMS and VisitBritain-led work through the Tourism Industry Emergency Response group (TIER) helped the London and UK tourism industries to achieve full recovery from the effects of the terrible bomb attacks of July 2005. In 2006, 32.2 million visitors spent a record £15.4 billion in the UK. TIER has established a robust and flexible response mechanism for dealing with tourism emergencies, which has already demonstrated its effectiveness during the bird flu scares of mid-2006 and early 2007. The strong industry performance which TIER helped maintain during 2006 provides a firm base for the economy to make the most of the historic visitor opportunity of the 2012 Olympic Games and Paralympic Games.

Gambling Act

Significant progress has been made towards implementing the Gambling Act 2005. In December 2006 this culminated in the publication of statutory instruments that enable the Gambling Commission to start accepting applications for new operating and personal licences. These will come into effect from 1 September 2007. Any business that wants to provide facilities for gambling in Britain will be licensed by the Commission. We consulted extensively with industry to ensure that secondary legislation reflects business needs. This took into account views on a range of issues, including the fees structure and a special exemption for small-scale operators, freeing them from the burden of having to acquire a personal licence.

DCMS also designed the transitional arrangements to minimise burdens on business – offering an appropriate notice period before applications are due; introducing a fast-track procedure for most existing businesses; letting existing licences for low-risk industry sectors roll over until expiry; and providing safety valve business continuation rights for applications not determined by 1 September 2007.

Above: Capturing the imagination of the travelling public, *England Rocks!* encouraged international and UK tourists to enjoy English locations and destinations associated with the country's rock and pop music heritage.

Cultural tourism

Oxford Castle is a unique,
award-winning visitor experience.
Features include the renovated
castle and prison, a new learning
centre and several cafés
and restaurants.

Names:	Haeree, Sang-hee and Junghyun
Location:	Oxford Castle, Oxford

'This is a great place to
chill and hang out. Kind
of escaping the city right
in its centre.'

'I love playing music with my friends. It's much more fun'

Live music

The music industry is a significant contributor to the UK's economy, producing £6 billion annually and employing about 130,000 people. In 2006, a combination of both new and established artists helped UK acts claim their largest share of album best-sellers since 1997. 66.9 million singles were sold in 2006 – the highest number since 1999 – of which 79 per cent were digital downloads. 2.2 million digital albums were sold between April and December 2006. The live music scene makes a vital contribution to that success.

The Live Music Forum, chaired by Feargal Sharkey, has continued to monitor the impact of the 2003 Licensing Act on the provision of live music and has considered ways in which live music, and its cultural and economic importance, can be further promoted. In 2006, the Forum and the Department jointly commissioned research into the experience of smaller venues in applying for authorisation under the 2003 Act to stage live music. The results of this research will help to inform the Forum when it produces its final recommendations to the Government in a few months' time.

Louie
Age 6

Britten Sinfonia
family music day,
Norwich

Creative Economy Programme

The Creative Economy Programme – a joint initiative between DCMS and the Department of Trade and Industry (DTI) – is the first comprehensive UK Government assessment of the state of our creative economy.

Within the programme, we are bringing together ideas from a broad range of stakeholders. These include seven working groups established at the outset of the programme, which examine the drivers of productivity in the creative economy, along with consultation responses and a schedule of industry consultation events.

Following further widespread industry consultation, we plan to produce a Green Paper in summer 2007. This will set out what makes the creative economy so important to the UK, how the creative sectors are changing, the drivers behind that change, and the potential obstacles to productivity in the sectors. It will have implications for Government policy and help identify how we best support the continued success of the creative economy in areas including education and skills, business support, technological development, and supporting the UK's cultural and economic infrastructure.

Tax relief for film

In November 2006, the European Commission approved a revised cultural test for British Film, in line with the European Union's State Aid requirements. As the first gateway to the new tax film reliefs announced by the Chancellor in the 2006 Budget, this is designed to encourage the production of culturally British films. Under the new relief, British films which pass the cultural test, spend more than 25 per cent of their expenditure in the UK, and are destined for theatrical release, will be eligible to claim relief worth up to 16 per cent of their budget for larger films and 20 per cent for smaller films. HM Treasury estimates the new tax relief will be worth as much as £120 million per year to the film industry.

The test has been widely welcomed by those working in the film sector. It consists of four key sections, each of which measures the extent of a film's British cultural character. Films will be awarded points in each of the categories, needing to score a minimum of 16 points out of a possible 31 to pass the test.

DCMS has also continued to make progress on negotiations on a new package of film co-production agreements, bringing economic and cultural benefits for the UK and partner countries. A treaty with South Africa, signed by the Secretary of State and the South African Arts Minister in May 2006, will come into force once the constitutional procedures have been completed. Negotiations are also progressing with India, China, Jamaica and Morocco. Such agreements enable films made jointly by UK producers and their counterparts in other countries to qualify as films with 'national' status in both the UK and the other country, meaning that they are eligible for any national incentives.

Top: *Bridge* by Michael Cross, part of the London Design Festival 2006.

Above: Ken Russell in conversation at the 2006 Encounters Short Film Festival in Bristol. Over 100 UK short films were shown at the festival.

Soulful singing

LSO St Luke's Community Choir is part of LSO Discovery, the London Symphony Orchestra's music education and community programme. With supporters including Arts Council England and Big Lottery Fund, the programme brings over 30,000 people annually into contact with the Orchestra, its music and musicians.

Names: Fotini and Nevo
Location: LSO St Luke's, London

'Singing is like air for me, it keeps me alive! I love working together each week. After our last concert, I was incandescent with joy – what an exhilarating experience!'

Performance and delivery

Public Service Agreements

Public Service Agreements (PSAs) set out each Department's aim, objectives and key outcome-based targets. They are agreed with HM Treasury and form an integral part of the spending plans outlined in Spending Reviews (SRs).

SR2002 PSA Target Summary

PSA 1

Enhance the take-up of sporting opportunities by 5-16 year olds by increasing the percentage of school children who spend a minimum of two hours each week on high quality PE and school sport within and beyond the curriculum from 25% in 2002 to 75% by 2006.

Performance summary
Met.

Indicator
Percentage of 5-16 year olds in schools who spend a minimum of two hours each week during term time on high quality PE and sport within and beyond the National Curriculum.

Proportion of lessons in which the quality of teaching is assessed by Ofsted as good or better.

Joint target with the Department for Education and Skills

PSA 2

Increase significantly take-up of cultural and sporting opportunities by new users aged 20 and above from priority groups.

Performance summary
Partly met.

Indicator
■ Take-up of arts opportunities by disabled people, black and ethnic minorities.

Performance summary: Not met.

■ Adult visitors from socio-economic C2, D and E groups to DCMS sponsored museums and galleries.

Performance summary: Met.

■ Visits to regional museums by new users.

Performance summary: Met.

■ Sport Coaching.

Performance summary: Partly met.

■ Visits by new users from minority and socially deprived groups to the historic environment.

Performance summary: Met.

PSA 3

Improve the productivity of the tourism, creative and leisure industries.

Performance summary
Met.*

Indicator
Productivity is estimated for each of the three industries by dividing gross value added by total employment. Gross value added and total employment are estimated from the Office of National Statistics Annual Business Inquiry. Baselines and targets are reported under two headings: 'Tourism and leisure-related industries' and 'Creative industries'. Targets take the form of annual percentage increases in the productivity figures higher than those for the service sector as a whole.

* Provisional data

PSA 4

Improve significantly the value for money of the Department's sponsored bodies, measured by a matrix of NDPB indicators.

Performance summary
Met.

Indicator
A range of performance indicators for two groups of sponsored bodies – the national museums and galleries and the Lottery distributors – will be collected and supplemented with text to explain any factors beyond an organisation's control that may explain variances. The outturn figures and text will be used to assess overall effectiveness and efficiency in delivering objectives.

Note that formal reporting against this set of indicators has been overtaken by the efficiency programme, reported on page 51.

PSA 1 Target

Enhance the take-up of sporting opportunities by 5-16 year olds by increasing the percentage of school children who spend a minimum of two hours each week on high quality PE and school sport within and beyond the curriculum from 25% in 2002 to 75% by 2006. (The 2002 baseline was an estimate of PE and school sports participation. The 2003-04 PE, School Sport and Club Links survey results are therefore used as the baseline.)

PE and school sport

Indicator

Percentage of 5-16 year olds in schools who spend a minimum of two hours each week during term time on high quality PE and sport within and beyond the National Curriculum. (Source: PE, School Sport and Club Links (PESSCL) Survey.)

Baseline: 62% of pupils in school sport partnerships participated in at least two hours of PE and school sport during 2003-04. (At the time of the survey 30% of schools in England were in a partnership.)

Ofsted evidence is also used to measure this PSA.

Project description

This is a programme of nine linked projects, collectively delivering the PE, School Sport and Club Links (PESSCL) Strategy. It is being delivered through an extensive network of delivery agents and partnerships. Those programmes are:

- Specialist sports colleges
- School Sport Partnerships
- Gifted and Talented
- QCA PE and School Sport Investigation
- Step into Sport
- Professional development
- Club links
- Swimming
- Sporting playgrounds

Linked work on coaching will also support delivery and forms part of the PSA 2 programme.

Progress

Met.

- The 2006 target has been exceeded by five percentage points.
- Ongoing work in this area is described under PSA 1 in SR2004.

Latest outturn data

The 2005-06 school sport survey showed that 80% of pupils within a School Sport Partnership took part in at least two hours of high quality PE and school sport in a typical week, compared with 69% in 2004-05. Participation in PE and sport in all three types of schools has also exceed the milestone: 82% of pupils in primary and special schools are doing at least two hours of high quality PE and Sport compared to 64% in 2004-05. The secondary schools figure is 78% compared with 75% in 2004-05.

There has also been a year-on-year improvement in all of the other key outcomes:

- 37% of pupils in partnership schools now take part in inter-school competitive sport, compared with 25% in 2003-04;
- 27% of pupils in partnership schools participate in club sport, a rise of 42% on 2003-04; and
- 13% of Year 10-13 pupils in partnerships schools are actively involved in sports leadership and volunteering.

From September 2006, all maintained schools in England have been within a school sport partnership and there are over 400 specialist sports colleges.

Ofsted judged that in 2003-04, the quality of teaching was good or better in 80% of secondary schools and 60% of primary schools.

Source of data: The 2005-06 PE, School Sport and Clubs Link (PESSCL) Survey and Ofsted reports

PSA 2 Target

Increase significantly take-up of cultural and sporting opportunities by new users aged 20 and above from priority groups.

This target is measured by a basket of five indicators covering culture and sports, as described below. The technical note stated that the minimum requirement to demonstrate progress toward the PSA target would be to meet four out of the six targets set. To date, we have met three targets on museums and heritage participation, and are on course for a fourth on sports participation (final results to be reported in the Department's Annual Report 2007). We did not meet the two targets on arts participation. The overall target is therefore partly met.

The Arts

Indicator
Increase attendance and participation by under-represented groups in arts events.

Targets: Increase attendance by 3% and participation by 2%.

Project description
The package of interventions underpinning this objective was delivered by Arts Council England (ACE), managed and monitored through the Funding Agreement with DCMS. ACE worked through three main funding channels: regularly funded organisations (RFOs), grants for the arts (open application funds) and flexible funds (which are not open to application).

Progress
Not met.

ACE has put a remedial action plan in place for the SR2004 PSA which builds on a number of key lessons learnt from delivery of this PSA. These include:

- a single system which will improve the way ACE captures PSA data;

- development of a toolkit to support RFOs in measuring their impact;

- establishment of a PSA 3 board within ACE;

- a restructured national office with the capacity and expertise to deliver on the PSA plan; and

- contributions to the *Taking Part* survey which allows greater consistency, accuracy and frequency of PSA data.

DCMS has established a strengthened PSA 3 Arts Advisory Board comprising key contacts from the voluntary, public and private sector who could influence the target and part of the wider delivery network. ACE is playing a major contributory role in this.

Latest outturn data
Analysis indicates that there has been no change in attendance or participation in the arts for any priority group.

There has been no statistically significant change for any priority group for either attendance or participation in the arts. The comparison is indicative as it is based on estimates adjusted to account for differing base and outturn data sources. The baselines for this target were set using the Omnibus Survey run by the Office for National Statistics. The 2001 survey provided baselines for the disabled and socially excluded elements of the target and the 2002 survey provided the baseline for the BME component. The target is being evaluated using data from the new DCMS *Taking Part* survey. In order to ensure consistency questions were asked simultaneously on both the Omnibus and *Taking Part* survey over

the same periods. This enabled the two data collection systems to be calibrated. A full report on the methodology for this is available on the DCMS website.

Comparing the engagement rate for the total population produced a calibration factor of 1.0 for the participation target and 1.1 for the attendance target. Applying these to the 2005/2006 *Taking Part* data showed that, for the resulting adjusted estimates, there has been no statistically significant change for any priority group for either attendance or participation.

National museums and galleries

Indicator
Increase by 8% by 2005-06 adult visitors in socio-economic groups C2, D and E to DCMS-sponsored national museums and galleries.

Project description
The maintenance of free access is key to further growth in admissions from these groups. The Funding Agreements for 2003-06 set specific targets for the groups concerned and each museum undertook specific targeted activities depending on its own circumstances. The outcomes of all of these projects were measured and evaluated.

Progress
Met.

Outturn data
Performance data collected from DCMS-sponsored museums and galleries.

C2DE visitors to national museums and galleries:

2002/03 Baseline	5,362,167
Target	5,791,140 (8%)
Latest outturn	6,820,939 (27%)

Regional museums

Indicator

Attract 500,000 visits to regional museums by new users.

Project description

£60m was available over the Spending Review period for building the capacity of groups of Hub museums in the nine regions, so that they could extend their reach to under-represented groups and step up their educational activities. The funds were administered by the Museums, Libraries and Archives Council under a framework agreed with DCMS. Development was in two phases, with the three Phase 1 Hubs receiving 70% of the SR2002 funds.

Progress

Met.

Latest outturn data

Performance data are provided by the Museums, Libraries and Archives Council.

This project started from a zero base.

2004-06

Total new users for the first two years of the target has been 3,086,283, of which 1,263,403 were from priority groups.

Sport

Indicator

Sport Coaching:

- National Coaching Certificate in 20 sports by 2006.
- 45 Coach Development Officers by 2005.
- 3,000 Community Sports Coach posts by 2006.

Project description

This project aimed to create a step change in the recruitment, education, employment and deployment of coaches working in England and elsewhere in the UK. It sought to transform coach education, professionalise and diversify the coaching workforce and open up access to enable many more people to benefit from coaching.

Progress

Partly met.

- 5-level UK Coaching Certificate (UKCC) framework established.
- 13 sports endorsed to deliver UKCC qualifications.
- Estimated that 18 sports will be endorsed to deliver UKCC qualifications by April 2007 and 21 by June.
- Network of 45 Coach Development Officers established by 2005.
- Created 3,000 Community Sports Coach (CSC) posts by end of 2006.

Latest outturn data

Performance data were provided by Sports Coach UK:

February 2007 – 33 Coach Development Officer (CDO) posts out of a total of 45 posts are currently filled. Appointments for vacant posts have been frozen while the CDO role is reviewed.

February 2007 – Funding awards made to support 3,248 CSC posts and 2,822 CSC posts currently filled.

Historic environment

Indicator

Attract 100,000 visits by new users from minority and socially deprived groups to the historic environment.

Project description

This project aimed to produce a step change in the way the sector managed engagement with the historic environment, including a more inclusive approach to site interpretation and the development of offers, which appealed to different sections of the community.

The target formed part of the English Heritage Funding Agreement. Delivery of the entire target was formally delegated to English Heritage.

Priority groups for this target were defined as Black and Minority Ethnic (BME) and social groups C2, D and E who had not visited an historic attraction in the last 12 months, as measured by self-declaration.

Progress

Met.

Latest outturn data

Performance data are provided by English Heritage.

The project started from a zero base.

2004-05 Outturn	323,478

PSA 3 Target

Improve the productivity of the tourism, creative and leisure industries.

The DCMS seeks to support this objective at a microeconomic level, with projects designed to impact on its sponsored industries. These take two forms: research aimed at understanding drivers of performance in the industries; and policies informed by the research and other evidence.

The impact of these projects will be measured and assessed through analysis of the contribution the tourism, creative and leisure industries make to UK productivity. This will be a long-term project. The base year for the data on productivity performance is 2002, and the trends in productivity up to and including 2005 are shown in the graph below.

The performance of each of the projects supporting the target was reported in the DCMS *Autumn Performance Report 2005*. Projects included overhauling legislation (the Communications Act 2003, the Licensing Act 2003 and the Gambling Act 2005); production of the Digital Television Action Plan; and tourism marketing activities. In each case, the aims for the project had been **met** in 2005. This information is therefore not repeated here.

The final results for this PSA will not be known until the data for 2005 becomes available in June/July 2007. The graph below and the table overleaf show that the target has been met for both creative industries and tourism and other leisure industries, however this result is based on provisional 2005 figures and is subject to change.

Latest outturn data
Overview

The graph below shows the change in productivity for creative industries, tourism and other leisure industries against the whole economy and service sector. The figures are shown as an index with a base year of 2002.

Indices of real changes in productivity

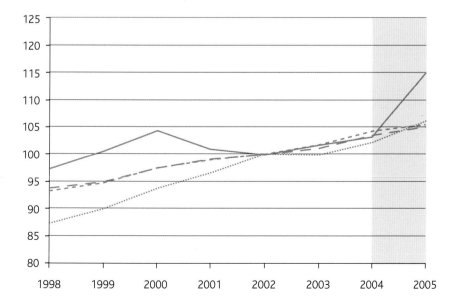

Provisional 2005 data show that productivity in both the creative industries and tourism and other leisure industries grew faster than for the service sector as a whole – in line with achieving the target.

However, this suggested rise is being investigated by the Office for National Statistics (ONS) and the data may be revised when the 2005 estimates are finalised in June/July 2007.

Productivity is measured as gross value added (GVA) divided by total employment (please see the Technical Note for more detail on definitions and methodology). The provisional 2005 data will be finalised in June/July 2007 so all data for that year should at this stage be acknowledged as provisional and could be subject to change.

Data are collated from ONS's Annual Business Inquiry (ABI). For more information please see: www.statistics.gov.uk/abi/default.asp ONS data are produced in accordance with National Statistics Code of Practice.

The data have some limitations when used to examine the reported changes in productivity:

- at low levels of disaggregation, the estimates from the ABI may fluctuate as a result of the sampling process and the complex way that Value Added is estimated;

- firms are classified by their main activity. The value added from any secondary activity will be allocated to their main category. This could lead to under- or over-estimates in some cases;

- to make meaningful comparisons across time it is necessary to ensure prices are constant. GVA figures are all expressed in 2002 prices, and an average annual gross domestic product deflator is used;

- GVA and employment from Standard Industrial Classification (SIC) codes are split to make the DCMS estimates of productivity. Constant proportions are used for tourism sectors such as bars, restaurants etc and creative industries;

- the Inter-Departmental Business Register (IDBR), used for Office for National Statistics business surveys, covers businesses that are registered for VAT. It will not include small businesses whose turnover is below the VAT threshold and who are not registered for VAT. The register will include businesses running a PAYE scheme. This means that coverage of businesses in some sectors of the creative industries will be limited.

Annual and average percentage productivity changes from 1998 onwards

Sector	1999	2000	2001	2002	2003	2004	2005	Average 1998-2005
Creative industries (excl design and craft)	3.3%	3.5%	-3.1%	-0.9%	1.5%	0.9%	12.4%	2.8%
Tourism-related and other leisure	3.0%	4.1%	3.2%	3.3%	-0.1%	1.6%	4.7%	3.3%
All services	1.2%	2.7%	1.7%	0.9%	1.2%	2.3%	1.6%	1.9%
Whole economy	1.6%	2.9%	1.5%	1.0%	1.8%	2.5%	1.1%	2.1%

Back series subject to change due to updates of the GDP Deflator.

PSA 4 Target

Improve significantly the value for money of the Department's sponsored bodies, measured by a matrix of NDPB indicators.

Progress
Met.

Under this PSA, a programme of work was devised to improve the value delivered through our sponsored bodies by:

- implementing targeted reform programmes for specific NDPBs where a major and pressing need has been identified;

- better aligning NDPB activity with DCMS priorities, through hold-back and ring fencing of funds and new tighter funding agreements;

- reforming the delivery of Lottery funds to ensure fairer and more cost-effective distribution to all areas and communities throughout the UK;

- improving our appointments function and the way in which we work with the Boards of our NDPBs; and

- identifying generic constraints on NDPB performance with which the Department can help, including those relating to pay and the workforce.

Seven related, though distinct, projects were set out in the DCMS 2004 *Autumn Performance Report* (APR). The 2005 APR reported that the reforms of the British Library, British Museum, Sport England, tourism bodies, and English Heritage had all been met early. The NDPB modernisation strategy had been subsumed into the Efficiency Programme set up as part of SR2004 (which is reported on below). The one project that had not been completed by the time of the 2005 APR was lottery reform. This has since been completed with the National Lottery Act 2006 receiving royal assent in July 2006.

Latest outturn data
As noted above, all projects undertaken in support of improving value for money in DCMS-sponsored bodies (as identified in 2004 APR) have been completed. Formal reporting against this set of indicators has been overtaken by the efficiency programme.

PSA 1

Enhance the take-up of sporting opportunities by 5-16 year olds so that the percentage of school children who spend a minimum of two hours each week on high quality PE and school sport within and beyond the curriculum from 25% in 2002 to 75% by 2006 and to 85% by 2008, and to at least 75% in each School Sport Partnership by 2008.

Performance summary
Ahead.

Indicator
Percentage of 5-16 year olds in schools who spend a minimum of two hours each week during term time on high quality PE and sport within and beyond the National Curriculum.

Joint target with Department for Education and Skills

PSA 2

Halt the year on year increase in obesity among children under 11 by 2010, in the context of a broader strategy to tackle obesity in the population as a whole.

Performance summary
On course.

Joint target with Department for Education and Skills and Department of Health

PSA 3

By 2008, increase the take-up of cultural and sporting opportunities by adults and young people aged 16 and above from priority groups.

Performance summary
Not yet assessed.

Indicator
- Increasing the number who participate in active **sports** at least 12 times a year by 3%, and increasing the number who engage in at least 30 minutes of moderate intensity level sport at least three times a week by 3%.

Performance summary:
Not yet assessed.

- Increasing the number who participate in **arts** activity at least twice a year by 2% and increasing the number who attend arts events at least twice a year by 3%.

Performance summary:
Not yet assessed.

- Increasing the number accessing **museums and galleries** collections by 2%.

Performance summary:
Not yet assessed.

- Increasing the number visiting designated **historic environment** sites by 3%.

Performance summary:
Not yet assessed.

PSA 4

By 2008 improve the productivity of the tourism, creative and leisure industries.

Performance summary
On course.*

Indicator
Productivity is estimated for each of the three industries by dividing gross value added by total employment. Gross value added and total employment are estimated from the Office of National Statistics Annual Business Inquiry (ABI). Baselines and targets are reported under two headings: 'Tourism and leisure-related industries' and 'Creative industries'. Targets take the form of annual percentage increases in the productivity figures higher than those for the service sector as a whole.

* Provisional data

PSA 1 Target

Enhance the take-up of sporting opportunities by 5-16 year olds by increasing the percentage of school children in England who spend a minimum of two hours each week on high quality PE and school sport within and beyond the curriculum from 25% in 2002 to 75% by 2006 and to 85% by 2008, and to at least 75% in each School Sport Partnership by 2008. (The 2002 baseline was an estimate of PE and school sports participation. The 2003-04 PE, School Sport and Club Links survey results are therefore used as the baseline.)

PE and school sport

Indicator

Percentage of 5-16 year olds in schools who spend a minimum of two hours each week during term time on high quality PE and sport within and beyond the National Curriculum. (Source: Annual Audit of School Sport Partnerships.)

Baseline: 62% of pupils in School Sport Partnerships participated in at least two hours of PE and school sport during 2003-04. (At the time of the survey 30% of schools in England were in a partnership.)

Ofsted evidence is also used to measure this PSA.

Project description

This is a programme of nine linked projects, collectively delivering the PE, School Sport and Club Links (PESSCL) Strategy. It is being delivered through an extensive network of delivery agents and partnerships. Those programmes are:

- Specialist sports colleges
- School Sports Partnerships
- Gifted and Talented
- QCA PE and School Sport Investigation
- Step into Sport
- Professional development
- Club links
- Swimming
- Sporting playgrounds

Progress
Ahead.

- 80% of pupils in School Sport Partnerships participated in at least two hours of PE and school sport during 2005-06. (At the time of the survey 80% of schools in England were in a partnership.)

- Since September 2006, all schools in England are within a School Sport Partnership.

- Take-up of professional development now exceeds monthly targets with over 100,000 teacher places taken up and driving high quality.

- The 2005-06 survey shows increased participation by girls and pupils with special needs.

- Participation by KS4 pupils, ethnic minorities and pupils from deprived backgrounds remains a challenge, as do regional variations.

Latest outturn data

The 2005-06 school sport survey showed that 80% of pupils within a School Sport Partnership took part in at least two hours of high quality PE and school sport in a typical week, compared with 69% in 2004-05. Participation in PE and sport in all three types of schools has also exceeded the milestone (82% of pupils in primary and special schools are doing at least two hours of high quality PE and Sport compared to 64% in 2004-05. The secondary schools figure is 78% compared with 75% in 2004-05).

There has also been a year-on-year improvement in all of the other key outcomes:

- 37% of pupils in partnership schools now take part in inter-school competitive sport, as compared with 25% in 2003-04;

- 27% of pupils in partnership schools participate in club sport, a rise of 42% on 2003-04; and

- 13% of Year 10-13 pupils in partnerships schools are actively involved in sports leadership and volunteering.

From September 2006, all maintained schools in England have been within a School Sport Partnership and there are over 400 specialist sports colleges.

The target of 75% of pupils in School Sport Partnerships doing two hours high quality PE and school sport was a 'floor' target. Now that all schools are within a School Sport Partnership, next year's survey will allow assessment of whether all partnership schools are above the 75% minimum target and look at the average across the partnerships.

Source of data: The 2005-06 school sport survey and Ofsted reports

PSA 2 Target

Halt the year-on-year increase in obesity among children under 11 by 2010, in the context of a broader strategy to tackle obesity in the population as a whole.

Childhood obesity

Indicator
Prevalence of obesity as defined by National BMI percentile classification for children aged 2-10 years (inclusive) measured through the Health Survey for England.

Halting the increase would mean no statistically significant change in prevalence between the two three-year periods, 2005/06/07 and 2008/09/10.

Project description
A comprehensive cross-Government programme of work to help families lead healthier and more active lives.

Progress
On course.

As a Department we have made good progress in helping families lead healthier and more active lives:

- in school sport (in partnership with the Department for Education and Skills), 80% of school children now do at least two hours of school sport a week, beating our target of 75% for 2006;

- we have published *Time for Play: encouraging greater play opportunities for children and young people;*

- Ofcom recently published their new rules on restricting the broadcast advertising of foods high in fat, salt and sugar to children.

Latest outturn data
Progress against the target is measured by the Health Survey for England (HSE) of obesity prevalence in children aged 2-10. Annual performance measured by comparing HSE figures for aggregate three-year periods (i.e. 2002-04 against 2003-05, against 2004-06 and so on until 2008-10.) Three-year aggregates are used to account for the limited sample size. The prevalence of obesity in 2-10 year old English children for the three-year period 2002-04 was 14.9%. The equivalent figure for 2003-05 was also 14.9%.

PSA 3 Target

By 2008, increase the take-up of cultural and sporting opportunities by adults and young people aged 16 and above from priority groups.

Participation in sport

Indicator

Increasing the number of people from priority groups who participate in active sports at least 12 times a year by 3%, and increasing the number who engage in at least 30 minutes of moderate intensity level sport at least three times a week by 3%. For this sub-target, priority groups are defined as women, people with a disability, people from lower socio-economic groups, and people from ethnic minorities.

Project description

About two-thirds of men and three-quarters of women do less than the recommended 30 minutes of moderate intensity activity a day on at least five days per week. The less well off are less active. Some regions of the UK are significantly less active than others. Through this target we aim to tackle these trends.

This target will be delivered through Sport England. The range of interventions comprises:

- marketing sport and promoting its benefits;
- building capacity in the network of development/outreach workers, clubs, coaches and volunteers;
- building infrastructure through innovative facilities projects;
- improving performance measurement at local level, notably through the *Active People* survey;
- driving up standards of local authority service provision through CPA/LAA/LPSA mechanisms; and
- locally driven partnership projects targeted at hard-to-reach groups.

Progress

Not yet assessed.

- Sport England Delivery Plan in place.
- New Funding Agreement, with strong focus on the PSA target agreed.
- *Active People* survey results published in December 2006 provide a detailed picture of participation at regional and local levels.

Latest outturn data

Not yet assessed.

This target will be measured by the Department's new survey, *Taking Part*. In December 2006, the baseline for each priority group was set as below.

The first indication of progress against the baseline will be available in summer 2007. It will be published on the *Taking Part* website.

Participation in active sport by priority group during the past four weeks

	At least one active sport (%)	Percentage range*
Black and minority ethnic	53.3	51.1-55.5
Limiting disability	32.3	31.0-33.6
Lower socio-economic	43.4	42.3-44.5
Women	47.7	46.7-48.7
All adults	**53.7**	**53.0-54.5**

* Using 95% confidence interval. Figures have been rounded to one decimal place

Participation in moderate intensity level sport by priority group during the last week

	At least one active sport (%)	Percentage range*
Black and minority ethnic	19.2	17.5-20.9
Limiting disability	9.5	8.7-10.3
Lower socio-economic	15.2	14.4-16.0
Women	18.5	17.7-19.3
All adults	**20.9**	**20.3-21.6**

*Using 95% confidence interval. Figures have been rounded to one decimal place

Participation in the arts

Indicator

Increasing the number of people from priority groups who participate in arts activity at least twice a year by 2% and increasing the number who attend arts events at least twice a year by 3%. For this sub-target, priority groups are defined as people with a disability, people from lower socio-economic groups, and people from ethnic minorities.

Project description

Breaking down barriers to access and exploiting the full wealth of UK culture have been key to our strategies in recent years.

This target will primarily be delivered through Arts Council England (ACE), but we are also engaging with non-DCMS delivery agents to increase participation across the sector as a whole.

The ACE delivery strand comprises the following key elements:

- the utilisation of funding agreements with Regularly Funded Organisations (RFOs) and in turn with third tier organisations to drive progress in delivery for priority groups;

- targets for Lottery Capital and Grants for the Arts distribution;

- development of better business models for arts organisations, including strategies for increasing participation and attendance at arts events by priority groups; and

- dissemination of lessons learnt and best practice from previous pilot programmes such as Decibel and the *New Audiences Programme*, which was a national action research programme (1998-2004) designed to test new approaches to building and reaching new audiences, and from new pilots as appropriate.

Progress
Not yet assessed

- Revised and strengthened ACE delivery plan incorporates lessons learned from the experience of SR2002 PSA 2.

- New funding agreement aligns ACE and DCMS strategic priorities with a clear focus on PSA 3.

- DCMS has commissioned a 'demand side' research project to improve understanding of involvement, participation and demand in arts and culture sectors which will be followed by practical interventions.

Latest outturn data
Not yet assessed.

This target will be measured by the Department's new survey, *Taking Part*. In December 2006, the baseline for each priority group was set as below.

The first indication of progress against the baseline will be available in summer 2007. It will be published on the *Taking Part* website.

Attendance at arts events by priority group during the past 12 months

	At least two events (%)	Percentage range*
Black and minority ethnic	23.5	21.6-25.4
Limiting disability	24.1	22.8-25.3
Lower socio-economic	17.4	16.6-18.3
All adults	**33.7**	**32.9-34.4**

*Using 95% confidence interval. Figures have been rounded to one decimal place

Participation in arts activities by priority group during the past 12 months

	At least two activities (%)	Percentage range*
Black and minority ethnic	20.8	19.1-22.5
Limiting disability	18.9	17.8-20.1
Lower socio-economic	15.3	14.5-16.1
All adults	**24.1**	**23.4-24.8**

*Using 95% confidence interval. Figures have been rounded to one decimal place

Accessing museums and galleries

Indicator

Increasing the number of people from priority groups accessing museums and galleries collections by 2%. For this sub-target, priority groups are defined as people with a disability, people from lower socio-economic groups, and people from ethnic minorities.

Project description

We will continue to build on the successful *Renaissance in the Regions* framework and the work of the national museums and galleries programmes in increasing museum visits and broadening audiences.

This will be strengthened by closer working with museums outside of the DCMS-sponsored museums to share best practice and develop joint programmes.

We will continue to build on the progress that has been achieved to date by:

- continuing to deliver 'Renaissance' across to the Hub museums and so increasing further the number of visits from priority groups;

- continuing to work with sponsored national museums and galleries to pursue particular programmes aimed at priority groups; and

- building on work with sponsored national museums and galleries to foster partnerships with museums and galleries in the regions aimed at encouraging participation from priority groups.

Progress

Not yet assessed.

- DCMS continues to chair project board meetings with Library Association and museum representation.

- Mid-year review of Funding Agreements is addressing the issue of establishing specific performance indicators for disability targets amongst national museums.

- DCMS has commissioned a 'demand side' research project to improve understanding of involvement, participation and demand in arts and culture sectors which will be followed by practical interventions.

Latest outturn data

Not yet assessed.

This target will be measured by the Department's new survey, *Taking Part*. In December 2006, the baseline for each priority group was set as below.

Attendance at museums and galleries by priority group during the past 12 months

	At least one visit (%)	Percentage range*
Black and minority ethnic	35.5	33.1-37.8
Limiting disability	32.1	30.8-33.5
Lower socio-economic	28.3	27.3-29.3
All adults	42.3	41.6-43.1

*Using 95% confidence interval. Figures have been rounded to one decimal place

The first indication of progress against the baseline will be available in summer 2007. It will be published on the *Taking Part* website.

1 December 2006 marked the fifth anniversary of free entry to national museums and galleries. There has been an 83% increase in all visits (not just from priority groups) to formerly charging museums since 2001, representing an extra 6.5 million visits in 2006.

Accessing historic environments

Indicator
Increasing the number of people from priority groups visiting designated historic environment sites by 3%. For this sub-target, priority groups are defined as people with a disability, people from lower socio-economic groups, and people from ethnic minorities.

Project description
English Heritage (EH) as DCMS's NDPB will work across the sector to provide support both to the sector and DCMS to deliver the target.

EH will continue to attract new users to the historic and built environment through established marketing and events, which are proven to be the most effective drivers for increasing access. EH will work to strengthen its links with non-DCMS sponsored heritage organisations to share best practice and develop joint programmes where possible.

This will be achieved through a variety of different programmes and activities:

- increasing visitor focus at English Heritage properties;

- using the expansion of Heritage Open Days and the Blue Plaques Scheme to broaden access at the local community level;

- attracting new visitors to English Heritage sites;

- specific projects run by English Heritage, including outreach, education and events programmes;

- national projects, including projects run by others but supported through English Heritage's grant programmes; and

- DCMS providing ministerial support for conferences and activities, i.e. *Your Place or Mine* and *Heritage Counts*.

Progress
Not yet assessed.

- EH's New Funding Agreement has a strong emphasis on the PSA target.

- DCMS has commissioned a 'demand side' research project to improve understanding of involvement, participation and demand in arts and culture sectors which will be followed by practical interventions.

Latest outturn data
Not yet assessed.

This target will be measured by the Department's new survey, *Taking Part*. In December 2006, the baseline for each priority group was set as below.

Attendance at designated historic environment sites by priority group during the past 12 months

	At least one visit (%)	Percentage range*
Black and minority ethnic	50.7	48.2-53.1
Limiting disability	59.5	58.0-61.0
Lower socio-economic	57.1	55.9-58.3
All adults	**69.9**	**69.1-70.6**

*Using 95% confidence interval. Figures have been rounded to one decimal place

The first indication of progress against the baseline will be available in summer 2007. It will be published on the *Taking Part* website.

PSA 4 Target

By 2008, improve the productivity of the tourism, creative and leisure industries.

The DCMS seeks to support this objective at a microeconomic level, with key projects designed to impact on its sponsored industries. These take two forms: research aimed at understanding drivers of performance in the industries; and policies informed by the research and other evidence.

The impact of these projects will be measured and assessed through analysis of the contribution the tourism, creative and leisure industries make to UK productivity. The final results for this PSA will not be known until the data for 2005 becomes available in June/July 2007. The graph and table on pages 37/38 show that the target has been met for both creative industries and tourism and other leisure industries, however this result is based on provisional 2005 figures and is subject to change.

Progress on projects that support the target is described below.

Implementation of the Licensing Act

Project description
This legislation reformed and streamlined archaic licensing laws, strengthening competition and increasing choice and flexibility for consumers while providing a greater degree of local and appropriate regulation and minimising harmful practices.

Progress
On course.

- The Act was implemented on 24 November 2005.

- 200,000 businesses have been operating under the new regime for over 12 months.

- The Fees Review Panel, set up to ensure that fees are set at the right level for local government and licensees, produced its final report at the end of November.

- Monitoring and evaluation of implementation underway since November 2005 – positive signs, though it remains too early to draw conclusions.

- Scrutiny councils initiative finalised – positive final report published in May 2006. The scrutiny council initiative involved a small, representative group of 10 licensing authorities to help DCMS monitor and evaluate the new regime.

- Initial guidance review is complete – the public consultation on the Main Review Guidance began in January and ended on 11 April 2007.

- Alcohol Strategy Group, chaired by the Home Office, is assessing progress with the Alcohol Harm Reduction Strategy.

- *Better Regulation Simplification Plan*, with key indicator baselines, was published in December 2006 and implementation is underway.

Implementation of the Gambling Act

Project description
When implemented, the Gambling Act will replace most existing gambling law. It will extend to the whole of Great Britain. It puts in place an improved, more comprehensive structure of gambling regulation, and creates a new independent regulatory body – the Gambling Commission.

Currently, we are working towards 1 September 2007 as the target date for full implementation of the Act. The main tasks that need to be completed to meet this target are:

- establishment of the Gambling Commission, its relocation to Birmingham and the development of its approach to regulation;

- Parliamentary approval for the secondary legislation necessary for full implementation of the Act;

- continued work with licensing authorities;

- establishment of an independent advisory panel that will provide advice to the Secretary of State about which licensing authorities should have the power to issue licences for casinos; and

- a programme of research into the prevalence of gambling and problem gambling, and its causes.

Progress
On course.

- The Gambling Commission was established in October 2005 and is operating effectively.

- The timetable for the programme of secondary legislation was published in April 2006.

- Programme management structures and governance are in place, geared towards close working with licensing authorities and industry stakeholders.

- The Independent Casino Advisory Panel established and operating effectively since October 2005. Secretariat strengthened in July 2006. The panel published its final report on 30 January 2007 and work is underway to secure the Parliamentary passage of the consequent secondary legislation.

- Gambling Prevalence Study 2006-07 underway and due to report in 2007.

- All the legislation necessary to allow both the Gambling Commission and Local Authorities to assume their main duties has now been laid.

Digital Switchover implementation

Project description
The Government is committed to achieving switchover in the UK by 2012, starting substantively in 2008 but with project Whitehaven in autumn 2007. It has also confirmed the region-by-region timetable and the scope of the Digital Switchover Help Scheme which will be established to help the over-75s and those with significant disabilities make the switch.

Digital UK, an independent organisation set up by the public sector broadcasters and multiplex operators with representation from the digital television supply chain, will co-ordinate the switchover to digital television.

Progress
On course.

- Digital UK fully established and operational.

- Programme structure and project plans for each work-strand are in place. Roles and responsibilities of each party agreed. Proactive approach to risk management embedded.

- Proportion of households that have adopted digital TV for at least one set stands at 73.3% (Ofcom Q3 2006 estimate).

- The Help Scheme work-strand is proceeding to procurement but details of the governance of the scheme will be settled as part of the conclusion of the BBC Licence Fee Settlement.

- Cost benefit analysis shows quantifiable customer benefits of around £1.1 – £2.2 billion in the period up to 2026 (in net present value).

Tourism projects

Project description
We are taking forward work with our delivery partners that will focus on investment, skills and competition, innovation and enterprise. Resulting projects will be complemented by a number of enabling programmes and other activities, which will provide us with knowledge, infrastructure and influence needed to underpin our Programme. Projects will be evaluated in light of their conclusions.

The work is being managed as a programme because of the complex interdependencies between the different projects. Although our overall success for the purposes of this PSA will be measured in terms of headline tourism productivity increases, it will not be possible to prove the cause and effect between one programme of work and certain amount of productivity gain.

Progress
On course.

- Complex delivery chains and interdependencies. Largely rests on the ability to influence other departments, local and regional partners and the industry.

- Overarching delivery programme plan in place, supported by individual project plans.

- Work on four strategic priority areas (marketing/e-tourism, quality, skills and data) progressing through to 2008.

- Tourism 2012 consultation launched and completed in November 2006, analysis of responses underway, and Strategy to be delivered from May 2007.

- Continuing work underway on how to measure the impact of DCMS interventions.

Creative industries projects

Project description

The Creative Economy Programme (CEP) was launched in November 2005. It aims to contribute to delivering increased productivity in creative industries sectors by identifying key interventions for Government. This includes:

- seven themed CEP working groups tasked with making recommendations to Government, looking at: competition and intellectual property, technology, diversity, business support and access to finance, education and skills, infrastructure, and evidence and analysis;

- extensive consultation including multiple industry consultation events and an online exercise to gather views from stakeholders and industry; and

- production of a strategy for better data on the creative sectors.

Additionally, the previously established, Intellectual Property Rights (IPR) and Film projects (including the Film Co-production Review) sit within the CEP.

The CEP has a complex and long delivery chain, with the sector mainly being comprised of small businesses.

Progress
On course.

- Connections are being made to other cross-Government work including the Business Support Simplification Programme, the Roberts Review on Creativity in Schools, the Cox report, the Technology Strategy Board and work on non-technological innovation.

- CEP will develop the strategic framework for delivering increased productivity.

- Working Group papers published in December 2006.

- Initial industry consultation events and an online consultation exercise have been completed and second round of industry summits now underway. CEP on track for publication of Green Paper in summer 2007.

- Work Foundation commission completed by April 2007.

Latest outturn data
The final results for this PSA will not be known until the data for 2005 becomes available in June/July 2007. The graph and table on pages 37/38 show that the target has been met for both creative industries and tourism and other leisure industries, however this result is based on provisional 2005 figures and is subject to change.

Taking Part

Taking Part is a continuous national survey, achieving an annual sample size of around 29,000, commissioned by the Department and its partner non-departmental public bodies (NDPBs). The fieldwork for *Taking Part* is being conducted by BMRB Social Research.

The data will allow robust measurement of the Departmental PSA target on increasing participation and attendance amongst priority groups. In the past, DCMS has not been able to report on progress against similar targets with the same level of confidence over accuracy that will be provided by *Taking Part*. The survey will also provide the data around which DCMS, our NDPBs and the wider cultural and sporting communities will be able to develop better research and analysis across our sectors.

Further details, including latest outputs, can be found on our website.

www.culture.gov.uk/reference_library/research/taking_part_survey/

Public Accounts Committee recommendations

Tackling childhood obesity

The Public Accounts Committee published its report on tackling childhood obesity on 25 January 2007.

www.publications.parliament.uk/pa/cm200607/cmselect/cmpubacc/157/15702.htm

A joint response from DCMS, the Department of Health and the Department for Education and Skills was published on 29 March 2007 on HM Treasury's website.

www.official-documents.gov.uk/document/cm70/7020/7020.asp

Efficiency

Efficiency gains

The table below illustrates DCMS's target to deliver £262 million of efficiency gains by 2007-08.

As agreed with HM Treasury and the Office for Government Commerce, data on efficiency gains are collected every six months from our NDPBs.

NDPBs' and Local Authorities' efficiency plans have been carefully scrutinised to ensure that proposed measures represent genuine efficiencies and not cuts in services. Similarly, different bodies' outputs (including productivity or quality measures) are also monitored to ensure that services are not being cut, as a result of the efficiency programme. Various measures will be used to ensure this, including progress towards meeting Public Service Agreement (PSA) targets, customer satisfaction surveys and Key Performance Indicators.

Further details are set out in the Department's Efficiency Technical Note and *Autumn Performance Report*, available on our website.

Headcount and relocation

DCMS has a target to reduce its own workforce by 27 posts (approximately 5%) by 2008 and to relocate 600 posts in its NDPBs outside London and the South East by 2010.

Headcount reductions will take place as part of the natural turnover of staff, without the need for redundancies. The relocation project has identified over 900 posts to be moved from London and the South East. As of 31 March 2007 DCMS has reduced headcount by 19 and has relocated 517 posts.

Further details are set out in our Efficiency Technical Note and *Autumn Performance Report*, available on our website.

Better Regulation

DCMS's Better Regulation Unit is a point of liaison between us and the Better Regulation Executive and aims to raise quality and standards across Departmental regulatory business. DCMS fully complies with the Cabinet Office's *Better Policy Making: A Guide to Regulatory Impact Assessments*. Regulatory Impact Assessments have been produced when required.

DCMS efficiency figures, £millions

Sector	2005-06 Gains	2006-07 Gains	2007-08 Target
Internal	0.0	1.0	2
NDPBs	73.0	130.7	114
of which			
Museums and galleries	34.9	52.9	45
Heritage	3.1	13.3	14
Strategic bodies	35.0	64.5	55
Local Authorities	44.7	84.6	146
Total gains	117.7	216.3	262

Capability review

DCMS was part of the third group of Government departments to undergo a capability review. These reviews are undertaken by the Prime Minister's Delivery Unit and an external Capability Review Team that includes successful, nationally recognised business and wider public sector leaders as well as board level members from other government departments. Their report was put to the DCMS Board on 31 January 2007 and the final report, including the DCMS response, was published on 27 March 2007.

We will take forward the findings of the review through our transformation action plan. This will enable us to say, by mid-2008, that:

- we understand clearly how we add value;

- the Department's leadership is decisive, corporate and visible;

- relationships with our NDPBs are based on strategic collaboration;

- staff are fully engaged in the transformation;

- we have reorganised DCMS to focus on where we add value and to support the new relationships with NDPBs; and

- we have improved how we recruit and allocate staff and how we manage their development.

The report and the DCMS transformation action plan can be found on the DCMS website.

www.culture.gov.uk/reference_library/ publications/archive_2007/capability_ review.htm

Correspondence figures

In July 2006 DCMS introduced a central Correspondence and Information Briefing Unit, to help improve the efficiency with which we handle requests for information.

DCMS received 9,102 letters from the public that required a response in 2006. 7,449 of these (81.8%) were answered within our 20 working day target. We also received 4,199 letters from MPs and Peers. 3,569 of these required a response, and 76.4% were answered within our 20 working day target.

Managing resources

Department for Culture, Media and Sport
Organisation chart April 2007

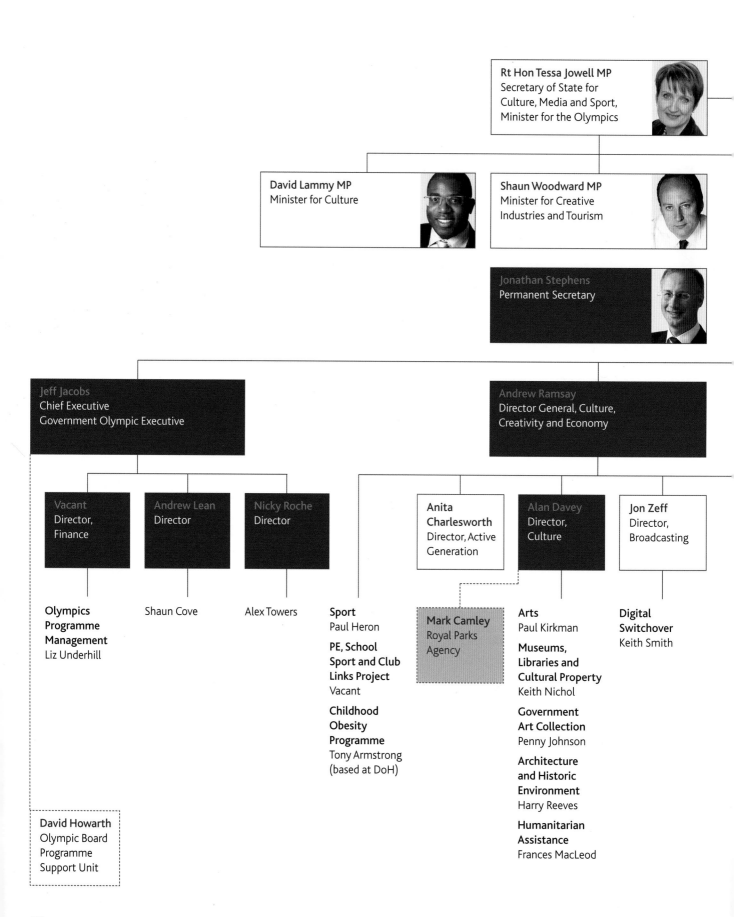

Rt Hon Tessa Jowell MP
Secretary of State for
Culture, Media and Sport,
Minister for the Olympics

David Lammy MP
Minister for Culture

Shaun Woodward MP
Minister for Creative
Industries and Tourism

Jonathan Stephens
Permanent Secretary

Jeff Jacobs
Chief Executive
Government Olympic Executive

Andrew Ramsay
Director General, Culture,
Creativity and Economy

Vacant
Director,
Finance

Andrew Lean
Director

Nicky Roche
Director

**Anita
Charlesworth**
Director, Active
Generation

Alan Davey
Director,
Culture

Jon Zeff
Director,
Broadcasting

**Olympics
Programme
Management**
Liz Underhill

Shaun Cove

Alex Towers

Sport
Paul Heron

**PE, School
Sport and Club
Links Project**
Vacant

**Childhood
Obesity
Programme**
Tony Armstrong
(based at DoH)

Mark Camley
Royal Parks
Agency

Arts
Paul Kirkman

**Museums,
Libraries and
Cultural Property**
Keith Nichol

**Government
Art Collection**
Penny Johnson

**Architecture
and Historic
Environment**
Harry Reeves

**Humanitarian
Assistance**
Frances MacLeod

**Digital
Switchover**
Keith Smith

David Howarth
Olympic Board
Programme
Support Unit

Nick Bent
Special Adviser

Nigel Warner
Special Adviser

Rt Hon Richard Caborn MP
Minister for Sport

Clive Elphick
Non-Executive Director

Parminder Vir
Non-Executive Director

Nicholas Holgate
Chief Operating Officer

Brian Leonard
Director,
Industry

David Roe
Director,
Strategy

Paddy Feeny
Director,
Communications

Patrick Kilgarriff
Director, Legal

**Gambling and
Lottery Licensing**
Matthew Hill

**Lottery,
Communities
and International**
Simon Broadley

Creative Industries
Phil Clapp

**Tourism, Economic
Impact and Licensing**
Andrew Cunningham

Public Bodies
Janet Evans

**Evidence
and Analysis**
Paula Crofts and
Ian Wood

**Human and
Business Resources**
Ros Brayfield

Private Office
Rita Patel

**Finance
and Planning**
Mark Ferrero

News
Linda Martin

Communications
Penny Dolby

Information Systems
Mark O'Neill

**Central Information
and Briefing Unit**
Harvey Vasey

Key

DCMS Agency:

DCMS Board member:

Policy Sponsorship:

Senior Civil Servants

Thirty-three Senior Civil Servants were in post at 1 April 2006. Details of their salaries are below:

Salary band £	Number of staff
£55,000 – 59,999	7
£60,000 – 64,999	6
£65,000 – 69,999	5
£70,000 – 74,999	2
Over £75,000	13

Recruitment

DCMS has systems in place to ensure that recruitment is carried out on the basis of fair and open competition and selection on merit, in accordance with the recruitment code laid down by the Civil Service Commissioners.

Further details about our recruitment process can be found on our website.

www.culture.gov.uk/working_with_us/recruitment/

Public appointments

DCMS is responsible for over 550 appointments to around six different boards. Most are national bodies with a high public profile and the majority are regulated by the Commissioner for Public Appointments.

Further details can be found in our Public Appointments Plan, available on our website.

www.culture.gov.uk/working_with_us/public_appointments/

Consultancy and publicity

Consultants bring a huge range of skills and experience to the Department and help support both the efficient administration and the programmes we deliver. DCMS spent £861,126 on consultancy in 2006-07 against a forecast of £825,000. Many projects that require consultants are arranged at short notice in order to address specific issues, making accurate forecasts difficult.

DCMS spent £714,443 on publicity in 2006-07.

Health and safety

The Health and Safety Committee continues to meet on a regular basis to receive reports from appointed officers, make recommendations and sanction future activities. Regular building inspections are carried out and any maintenance work with a health or safety requirement is given priority. First aid training is provided to volunteers and security guards.

Sustainable development

Our plans for implementing sustainable development within DCMS and among our sponsored bodies are set out in our first *Sustainable Development Action Plan*, published in March 2006. Progress against this action plan is overseen by the Director of Strategy, who is the DCMS Board sustainable development champion. The Sustainable Development Commission recently assessed the plan as 'gaining momentum'.

Further details can be found in the *Sustainable Development Action Plan*, available on our website. We will be publishing our *Sustainable Development Action Plan* for 2007-08 in June 2007.

www.culture.gov.uk/working_with_us/sustainable_development/

Equality and diversity

In December 2006, DCMS published its Equality Scheme, incorporating its Race Equality Scheme, Disability Equality Scheme, Gender Equality Scheme and Northern Ireland Equality Scheme. This sets out our action plan for equality and diversity. Progress against this action plan is overseen by the Director of Strategy, who is the DCMS Board diversity champion. The scheme was reviewed in advance of the gender duty coming into effect on 30 April 2007.

Further details, including employment statistics, can be found in the Equality Scheme, available on our website.

www.culture.gov.uk/working_with_us/equality_diversity.htm

Public bodies

As of 31 March 2007, DCMS is responsible for 63 public bodies that help deliver the Department's strategic aim and objectives. These include three public corporations, two public broadcasting authorities, one executive agency and 57 non-departmental public bodies (NDPBs). NDPBs fall into three categories: executive, advisory and tribunal. However, NDPB is often used within DCMS to mean all of our sponsored bodies. Over 95% of our expenditure is channelled through these bodies. A breakdown of grant-in-aid expenditure on our sponsored bodies is provided overleaf.

The relationship between DCMS and our public bodies is a balance between independence and accountability. Public bodies perform functions best carried out at arms length from government. For example, some are regulators, and must be seen to be independent of political interests. Others need specialised expertise not found in general public administration.

Public bodies also spend public money, from the Exchequer or from the National Lottery, and are therefore accountable to the public, Ministers and Parliament. While they should have a large measure of freedom to determine how they operate, they need to do so within the framework of policies and priorities developed by the sponsor department and agreed by Parliament.

That framework is encapsulated in the following key documents, one of more of which apply to most of our bodies:

- the Public Service Agreements (PSAs) set out our aims and objectives, which encompass the work of all our public bodies, and our key targets. Details of our PSAs can be found on page 33;

- the funding agreement supports the PSA by explaining what each body will deliver for the public funding allocated to it, and why; the agreement, signed every two years by the Chair of the body and the Secretary of State, summarises strategy, key activities, and outputs to be delivered;

- the management statement and financial memorandum sets out the rules and guidelines that a public body should observe in carrying out its functions; it is reviewed periodically, but the content remains fairly constant.

For the National Lottery distributing bodies, policy and financial directions and a statement of financial requirements set out rules on the treatment of Lottery proceeds, particularly where this differs from the treatment of Exchequer funds.

All the public corporations, public broadcasting authorities and executive NDPBs are required to produce annual reports and accounts that are either laid before Parliament or placed in the Library of the House of Commons.

Further information on these public bodies (including how to obtain copies of their annual report and accounts) and an explanation of the characteristics of the different types of public bodies can be found in the DCMS *Public Bodies Directory 2007* on the DCMS website.

www.culture.gov.uk/about_us/sponsored_bodies/

We share responsibility with the Department of Trade and Industry (DTI) for Ofcom (a public corporation) and the Design Council (an executive NDPB). Further information on these bodies can be found on the DTI website.

DCMS provides an annual grant of £16.1 million to the Royal Household for the maintenance of the Occupied Royal Palaces, for Royal Communications and Information and for the maintenance of Marlborough House. The Occupied Royal Palaces are the palaces currently used by The Queen or members of the Royal Family. These are:

- Buckingham Palace

- Windsor Castle

- St James's Palace

- Clarence House

- The residential areas of Kensington Palace

For more information visit the official website of the British Monarchy.

www.royal.gov.uk

Department for Culture, Media and Sport
Detailed allocation: NDPB grant-in-aid

£ Thousands	2005-06 Outturn	2006-07 Estimated Outturn	2007-08 Plans
Museums, galleries and libraries	**451,834**	**484,907**	**513,032**
of which:			
British Museum	39,856	42,929	44,823
Natural History Museum	41,470	44,082	45,090
Imperial War Museum	18,541	20,613	22,177
National Gallery	21,986	24,041	25,566
National Maritime Museum	15,236	17,008	18,411
National Museums Liverpool	18,155	21,203	21,576
National Portrait Gallery	6,448	7,031	7,168
National Museum of Science and Industry	34,113	39,225	38,484
Tate Gallery	31,799	34,124	35,929
Victoria & Albert Museum	38,233	39,112	41,777
Wallace Collection	2,580	3,528	4,156
Royal Armouries	7,369	7,814	8,312
Museum of Science and Industry in Manchester	3,870	4,215	4,171
Museum of London	6,632	7,931	8,809
Sir John Soane's Museum	1,291	1,115	1,008
Horniman Museum	3,682	3,932	4,350
Geffrye Museum	1,431	1,740	1,859
Tyne and Wear Museums	1,710	1,863	2,326
National Coal Mining Museum of England	2,539	2,528	2,659
People's History Museum	150	156	164
British Library	100,568	102,639	104,411
Public Lending Right	7,471	7,702	7,682
Museums, Libraries and Archives Council	14,264	15,793	14,521
Arts	**408,305**	**427,861**	**416,955**
of which:			
Arts Council England	408,305	422,361	410,455
Sport	**135,297**	**156,669**	**180,229**
of which:			
Sport England	104,627	102,500	115,963
UK Sports Council	29,305	52,995	63,005
Football Licensing Authority	1,365	1,174	1,261
London 2012 – Olympic Delivery Authority	**–**	**106,026**	**175,000**

£ Thousands	2005-06	2006-07	2007-08
Historic buildings, monuments and sites	**164,102**	**161,788**	**166,997**
of which:			
English Heritage	133,121	133,511	133,136
Churches Conservation Trust	3,062	3,062	3,062
National Heritage Memorial Fund	5,002	5,002	10,002
Commission for Architecture and the Built Environment	4,690	3,690	4,690
Royal Household	18,227	16,523	16,107
Tourism	**52,500**	**53,500**	**53,500**
of which:			
VisitBritain	48,900	49,900	49,900
Broadcasting and media	**31,660**	**29,480**	**27,010**
of which:			
UK Film Council	28,760	26,610	24,110
National Film and Television School	2,900	2,870	2,900
Regional Cultural Consortiums	**1,810**	**1,632**	**1,885**
National Lottery Commission	**7,562**	**9,200**	**14,001**
Gambling Commission	**12,132**	**18,741**	**4,220**

Department for Culture, Media and Sport
Resource budget: Departmental Expenditure Limit (DEL)

£ Thousands	2001-02 Outturn	2002-03 Outturn	2003-04 Outturn	2004-05 Outturn	2005-06 Outturn	2006-07 Estimated Outturn	2007-08 Plans
Resource DEL							
DCMS	1,006,102	1,227,239	1,224,728	1,325,784	1,422,398	1,624,668	1,563,766
of which:							
Museums, galleries and libraries	302,227	423,595	446,039	441,534	482,561	595,737	547,636
of which:							
Museums and galleries	172,640	281,973	313,272	310,509	364,077	405,465	414,357
Libraries	115,568	126,012	119,213	117,954	97,544	137,922	119,353
Museums, Libraries and Archives Council	13,104	15,357	12,776	12,218	18,283	49,777	13,926
Culture Online	915	253	778	853	2,657	2,573	–
Arts	254,161	285,740	328,618	366,955	406,851	424,490	420,751
Sport	67,381	122,594	66,143	106,459	120,646	155,210	170,130
of which:							
Sports and recreation	67,381	122,594	66,143	100,001	116,589	121,639	166,530
Olympics	–	–	–	6,458	4,057	33,571	3,600
Architecture and the historic environment	132,848	142,133	152,985	162,056	146,406	179,129	159,117
Regional Cultural Consortiums	–	–	–	1,501	1,650	1,910	1,885
The Royal Parks Agency	41,854	25,671	25,706	26,660	31,122	19,507	19,112
Tourism	68,250	73,446	53,039	50,349	51,202	51,808	54,424
Broadcasting and media	106,517	107,592	108,472	124,981	121,811	120,686	120,380
Commemorative services (Queen's Golden Jubilee)	417	6,494	–	–	–	–	–
Administration and research	33,176	37,914	41,546	42,393	48,515	54,514	50,759
Unallocated provision	–	–	–	–	4,829	8,954	17,039
Gambling and gaming bodies	-729	2,060	2,180	2,896	6,805	12,723	2,533
National Lottery	-350	130	-156	100	497	-238	181
Total resource budget DEL	1,005,752	1,227,369	1,224,572	1,325,884	1,422,895	1,624,430	1,563,947
of which:							
Near-cash	871,415	1,078,171	1,084,087	1,196,983	1,269,628	1,448,120	1,375,338
of which:†							
Pay	316,841	376,167	403,706	441,534	446,101	469,046	
Procurement	116,440	170,820	197,242	185,672	237,858	274,371	316,454
Current grants and subsidies to the private sector and abroad	359,317	438,967	397,922	475,660	489,234	589,316	571,502
Current grants to local authorities	2,000	12,000	–	1,900	4,218	23,145	3,477
Depreciation	74,414	68,861	67,522	52,340	80,311	97,771	101,730

Department for Culture, Media and Sport
Resource budget: Annually Managed Expenditure (AME)

£ Thousands	2001-02 Outturn	2002-03 Outturn	2003-04 Outturn	2004-05 Outturn	2005-06 Outturn	2006-07 Estimated Outturn	2007-08 Plans
Resource AME							
DCMS	2,230,000	2,534,030	2,963,763	2,487,054	2,537,000	2,722,000	2,811,000
of which:							
Museums, galleries and libraries	–	1,522	317,641	1,798	–	–	–
of which:							
Museums and galleries	–	–	1,747	1,798	–	–	–
Libraries	–	1,522	315,894	–	–	–	–
Sport	–	–	1,003	–	–	–	–
of which:							
Sports and recreation	–	–	1,003	–	–	–	–
Architecture and the historic environment	–	550	195,500	–	–	–	–
Tourism	–	1,381	-1,381	256	–	–	–
Broadcasting and media	2,230,000	2,530,577	2,451,000	2,485,000	2,537,000	2,722,000	2,811,000
National Lottery	897,880	651,694	662,237	608,038	789,772	713,504	628,070
of which:							
National Lottery	897,880	651,694	662,237	608,038	789,772	691,504	605,070
Olympic Lottery	–	–	–	–	–	22,000	23,000
Total resource budget AME	3,127,880	3,185,724	3,626,000	3,095,092	3,326,772	3,435,504	3,439,070
of which:							
Near-cash	3,109,798	3,148,734	3,613,952	3,084,974	3,342,587	3,409,928	3,408,001
of which:[†]							
Pay	712,000	764,000	804,619	843,000	825,000	834,000	
Procurement	1,818,000	2,167,000	2,139,381	2,157,256	2,279,000	2,383,000	2,435,000
Current grants and subsidies to the private sector and abroad	897,880	644,694	662,237	608,038	789,772	713,504	628,070
Current grants to local authorities	46,918	29,391	54,571	56,882	50,815	44,424	38,931
Depreciation	33,000	33,000	34,000	34,000	35,000	35,000	35,000
Total resource budget	4,133,632	4,413,093	4,850,572	4,420,976	4,749,667	5,059,934	5,003,017

Notes:

[†] The breakdown of near-cash in Resource DEL by economic category may exceed the total near-cash Resource DEL reported above because of other income and receipts that score in near-cash Resource DEL but aren't included as pay, procurement, or current grants and subsidies to the private sector, abroad and local authorities.

Figures in this table are in a new format separating Departmental Expenditure Limit (DEL) and Annually Managed Expenditure (AME). Overall figure may differ from previous years as a result of:

1. A change in the classification of profit and loss on the disposal of assets – amounts now recorded as Capital.

2. DCMS and Treasury undertook at complete overhaul of the way Lottery expenditure is recorded. For COFOG purposes each lottery distribution body is recorded separately, the exercise offered an opportunity to remove erroneously recorded data.

Please see additional notes on page 72.

Department for Culture, Media and Sport
Capital budget: Departmental Expenditure Limit (DEL)

£ Thousands	2001-02 Outturn	2002-03 Outturn	2003-04 Outturn	2004-05 Outturn	2005-06 Outturn	2006-07 Estimated Outturn	2007-08 Plans
Capital DEL							
DCMS	32,680	27,972	123,453	153,548	144,459	243,769	401,827
of which:							
Museums, galleries and libraries	17,964	-13,685	47,333	76,937	58,947	51,974	131,220
of which:							
Museums and galleries	5,122	-29,142	28,612	41,672	14,075	36,366	71,952
Libraries	1,686	5,715	2,165	7,900	10,513	12,083	27,218
Museums, Libraries and Archives Council	11,156	9,742	15,895	24,325	29,144	50	32,050
Culture Online	–	–	661	3,040	5,215	3,475	–
Arts	1,224	1,551	2,876	942	6,639	7,444	373
Sport	1,194	17,024	44,276	49,772	44,201	148,508	211,334
of which:							
Sports and recreation	615	6,924	3,238	22,189	6,413	46,977	36,334
Space for sports and arts	579	10,100	41,038	27,583	2,100	–	–
Olympics	–	–	–	–	35,688	101,531	175,000
Architecture and the historic environment	10,382	17,700	20,245	19,487	23,445	11,376	40,884
The Royal Parks Agency	118	1,425	4,987	2,562	1,463	555	1,880
Tourism	662	1,158	451	764	298	300	600
Broadcasting and media	400	1,738	2,040	739	3,072	8,392	2,040
Administration and research	735	1,061	1,220	2,345	5,820	10,315	4,495
Unallocated provision	–	–	–	–	–	–	9,000
Gambling and gaming bodies	1	–	25	–	574	4,905	1
National Lottery	489	57	72	–	67	62	10
Total capital budget DEL	33,169	28,029	123,525	153,548	144,526	243,831	401,837
of which:							
Capital expenditure on fixed assets net of sales[†]	13,202	-8,513	47,050	65,261	55,543	90,650	104,000
Capital grants to the private sector and abroad	–	–	–	–	–	–	–
Net lending to private sector	–	–	–	–	–	–	–
Capital support to public corporations	–	–	90	90	–	–	90
Capital support to local authorities[††]	–	–	–	10,045	39,373	105,191	175,147

**Department for Culture Media and Sport
Annual Report 2007**

Session 2006/2007

Cm 7104

ISBN 978 0 10 171042 8

CORRECTION

Please note the following corrections:

page 63:-

DCMS Capital AME for 2005-06 should read £104,000

Total Capital budget AME figure for 2005-06 should read £1,002,014

The Total Capital budget figure for 2005-06 should read £1,146,540

May 2007
LONDON: THE STATIONERY OFFICE

Department for Culture, Media and Sport
Capital budget: Annually Managed Expenditure (AME)

£ Thousands	2001-02 Outturn	2002-03 Outturn	2003-04 Outturn	2004-05 Outturn	2005-06 Outturn	2006-07 Estimated Outturn	2007-08 Plans
Capital AME							
DCMS	145,620	122,000	4,000	88,000	94,000	94,000	80,000
of which:							
Museums, galleries and libraries	26,620	10,000	10,000	10,000	10,000	10,000	10,000
of which:							
Museums and galleries	26,620	10,000	10,000	10,000	10,000	10,000	10,000
Broadcasting and media	119,000	112,000	-6,000	78,000	94,000	84,000	70,000
National Lottery	719,555	1,011,018	1,098,737	942,836	898,014	873,329	777,167
of which:							
National Lottery	719,555	1,011,018	1,098,737	942,836	898,014	785,329	687,167
Olympic Lottery	–	–	–	–	–	88,000	90,000
Total capital budget AME	865,175	1,133,018	1,102,737	1,030,836	992,014	967,329	857,167
Total capital budget	898,344	1,161,047	1,226,262	1,184,384	1,136,540	1,211,160	1,259,004
of which:							
Capital expenditure on fixed assets net of sales†	158,822	113,487	51,050	153,261	149,543	184,650	184,000
Less depreciation†††	107,414	101,861	101,522	86,340	115,311	167,771	136,730
Net capital expenditure on tangible fixed assets	51,408	11,626	-50,472	66,921	34,232	16,879	47,270

Notes:

† Expenditure by the department and NDPBs on land, buildings and equipment, net of sales. Excludes spending on financial assets and grants, and public corporations' capital expenditure.

†† This does not include loans written off by mutual consent that score within non-cash Resource Budgets.

††† Included in Resource Budget.

Figures in this table are in a new format separating Departmental Expenditure Limit (DEL) and Annually Managed Expenditure (AME). Overall figure may differ from previous years as a result of:

1. A change in the classification of profit and loss on the disposal of assets – amounts now recorded as Capital.

2. DCMS and Treasury undertook a complete overhaul of the way Lottery expenditure is recorded. For COFOG purposes each lottery distribution body is recorded separately, the exercise offered an opportunity to remove erroneously recorded data.

Please see additional notes on page 72.

Department for Culture, Media and Sport
Total departmental spending

£ Thousands	2001-02 Outturn	2002-03 Outturn	2003-04 Outturn	2004-05 Outturn	2005-06 Outturn	2006-07 Estimated Outturn	2007-08 Plans
Resource budget							
Resource DEL DCMS	1,006,102	1,227,239	1,224,728	1,325,784	1,422,398	1,624,668	1,563,766
National Lottery	-350	130	-156	100	497	-238	181
Total resource budget DEL	**1,005,752**	**1,227,369**	**1,224,572**	**1,325,884**	**1,422,895**	**1,624,430**	**1,563,947**
of which: Near-cash	871,415	1,078,171	1,084,087	1,196,983	1,269,628	1,448,120	1,375,338
Resource AME DCMS	2,230,000	2,534,030	2,963,763	2,487,054	2,537,000	2,722,000	2,811,000
National Lottery	897,880	651,694	662,237	608,038	789,772	713,504	628,070
Total resource budget AME	**3,127,880**	**3,185,724**	**3,626,000**	**3,095,092**	**3,326,772**	**3,435,504**	**3,439,070**
of which: Near-cash	3,109,798	3,148,734	3,613,952	3,084,974	3,342,587	3,409,928	3,408,001
Total resource budget	**4,133,632**	**4,413,093**	**4,850,572**	**4,420,976**	**4,749,667**	**5,059,934**	**5,003,017**
of which: depreciation	107,414	101,861	101,522	86,340	115,311	167,771	136,730
Capital budget							
Capital DEL DCMS	32,680	27,972	123,453	153,548	144,459	243,769	401,827
National Lottery	489	57	72	–	67	62	10
Total capital budget DEL	**33,169**	**28,029**	**123,525**	**153,548**	**144,526**	**243,831**	**401,837**
Capital AME DCMS	145,620	122,000	4,000	88,000	94,000	94,000	80,000
National Lottery	719,555	1,011,018	1,098,737	942,836	898,014	873,329	777,167
Total capital budget AME	**865,175**	**1,133,018**	**1,102,737**	**1,030,836**	**992,014**	**967,329**	**857,167**
Total capital budget	**898,344**	**1,161,047**	**1,226,262**	**1,184,384**	**1,136,540**	**1,211,160**	**1,259,004**
Total departmental spending[†]							
DCMS	3,307,824	3,807,509	4,212,488	3,965,330	4,075,277	4,499,602	4,717,433
National Lottery	1,616,738	1,664,770	1,762,824	1,553,690	1,695,619	1,603,721	1,407,858
Total departmental spending[†]	**4,924,562**	**5,472,279**	**5,975,312**	**5,519,020**	**5,770,896**	**6,103,323**	**6,125,291**
of which: Total DEL	964,507	1,186,537	1,280,575	1,427,092	1,487,110	1,770,490	1,864,054
Total AME	4,052,616	4,425,528	4,843,762	4,245,050	4,424,554	4,455,923	4,369,001
Spending by local authorities on functions relevant to the department							
Current spending	1,840,253	1,921,554	2,108,205	2,107,459	2,228,945	2,305,686	
of which: financed by grants from budgets above	48,918	41,391	54,571	58,782	55,033	67,569	
Capital spending	505,726	474,368	444,828	511,010	696,230	901,900	
of which: financed by grants from budgets above[††]	45,643	110,395	94,454	106,285	129,326	187,801	

Notes:

[†] Total department spending is the sum of the resource budget and the capital budget less depreciation. Similarly, total DEL is the sum of the resource budget DEL and capital budget DEL less depreciation in DEL, and total AME is the sum of resource budget AME and capital budget AME less depreciation in AME.

[††] This includes loans written off by mutual consent that score within non-cash Resource Budgets and aren't included in the capital support to local authorities line in Table 3.

Figures in this table are in a new format separating Departmental Expenditure Limit (DEL) and Annually Managed Expenditure (AME), and DCMS and Lottery expenditure. Overall figures may differ from previous year as a result of:

1. DCMS and Treasury undertook a complete overhaul of the way Lottery expenditure is recorded. For Classification of the Functions of Government (COFOG) purposes each lottery distribution body is recorded separately, the exercise offered an opportunity to remove erroneously recorded data.

Department for Culture, Media and Sport
Capital employed

£ Millions	2001-02 Outturn	2002-03 Outturn	2003-04 Outturn	2004-05 Outturn	2005-06 Outturn	2006-07 Estimated Outturn	2007-08 Plans
Assets on balance sheet							
Fixed assets	56	57	68	70	86	90	92
of which:							
Land and buildings	51	51	59	56	70	70	71
Debtors (> 1 year)					6	6	
Current assets	36	81	59	42	35	59	67
Creditor (< 1 year)	-29	-96	-76	-52	-38	-44	-77
Creditor (> 1 year)							
Provisions					-4	-4	
Capital employed within main department	63	42	51	60	85	107	82
NDPB net assets	1,697	1,870	3,237	3,260	3,861	3,962	4,063
Total capital employed in departmental group	**1,760**	**1,912**	**3,288**	**3,320**	**3,946**	**4,069**	**4,145**

Notes:

1. Outturn figures are taken from the published consolidated DCMS resource accounts which include the Royal Parks Agency accounts.

2. Figures for 2003-04 include the effects of the quinquennial revaluation of the land and buildings of the museums and galleries sector.

Department for Culture, Media and Sport
Administration budget

£ Thousands	2001-02 Outturn	2002-03 Outturn	2003-04 Outturn	2004-05 Outturn	2005-06 Outturn	2006-07 Estimated Outturn	2007-08 Plans
Adminstration expenditure							
Paybill	15,402	17,262	18,681	19,847	22,191	23,529	25,482
Other	16,639	19,107	22,909	22,789	26,968	28,121	25,673
Total admistration							
Expenditure	32,041	36,369	41,590	42,636	49,159	51,650	51,155
Administration income	-238	-241	-2,231	-2,151	-2,486	-1,003	-897
Total administration budget	**31,803**	**36,128**	**39,359**	**40,485**	**46,673**	**50,647**	**50,258**

£ million							
Analysis by activity							
Arts and culture	7	10	11	11	13	13	13
Sport	6	4	4	5	7	7	7
Government Olympic Executive	0	0	0	0	0	3	3
Tourism, libraries and communities	6	4	6	6	6	7	7
Creative industries, broadcasting and gambling	5	6	8	8	9	9	9
Administration	9	12	10	10	11	12	11
Total net administration costs	**33**	**36**	**39**	**40**	**46**	**51**	**50**

The real terms increase between 2001-02 and 2006-07 includes the creation of the Humanitarian Assistance Unit and the Government Olympic Executive.

Department for Culture, Media and Sport
Staff in post

Staff years	2001-02 Outturn	2002-03 Outturn	2003-04 Outturn	2004-05 Outturn	2005-06 Outturn	2006-07 Estimated Outturn	2007-08 Plans
DCMS							
FTEs	400	460	506	510	507	525	495
Overtime	12	10	12	10	12	10	10
Total	**412**	**470**	**518**	**520**	**519**	**535**	**505**
Royal Parks Agency							
FTEs	220	234	232	127	121	92	92
Overtime	9	10	7	4	2	2	2
Casual	0	7	3	3	1	5	4
Total	**229**	**251**	**242**	**134**	**124**	**99**	**98**

Notes:

1. Until 2002-03 FTE data consisted of the staff in post averaged over the whole financial year. From 2003-04 onwards the data represents the number of staff in post (FTE) on the last day of the financial year.

2. The Royal Parks Agency (RPA) ceased to be subject to administration cost control from 2003-04. The fall in RPA staff numbers from 242 in 2003-04 to 125 in 2005-06 is the result of a planned merger of the Royal Parks Constabulary (RPC) with the Metropolitan Police. After the merger, RPC staff will no longer be Royal Parks Agency.

3. Agency temps are excluded from the figures.

Department for Culture, Media and Sport
Total spending by country and region

£ Million	2001-02 Outturn	2002-03 Outturn	2003-04 Outturn	2004-05 Outturn	2005-06 Outturn	2006-07 Plans	2007-08 Plans
North East	167.3	134.4	179.4	155.0	141.5	131.5	118.4
North West	243.9	270.1	291.9	265.9	285.1	225.7	209.6
Yorkshire and Humberside	237.9	231.1	271.1	203.7	234.8	235.7	218.7
East Midlands	164.5	179.0	193.4	204.7	152.7	177.1	166.0
West Midlands	182.7	202.3	337.0	188.6	214.4	233.9	218.6
Eastern	184.1	166.4	194.8	180.8	175.2	186.5	173.7
London	464.6	561.3	804.8	508.9	649.9	748.8	720.0
South East	257.5	284.2	325.0	305.8	272.0	299.2	282.0
South West	177.9	219.4	261.2	300.3	215.4	282.0	256.5
Total England	**2,080.4**	**2,248.2**	**2,858.5**	**2,313.5**	**2,340.9**	**2,520.4**	**2,363.7**
Scotland	196.7	201.5	181.3	218.8	238.7	180.3	159.6
Wales	190.4	198.7	205.7	236.4	222.7	244.1	228.9
Northern Ireland	67.4	71.1	72.7	63.5	95.9	98.2	87.7
Total UK identifiable expenditure	**2,534.9**	**2,719.5**	**3,318.2**	**2,832.1**	**2,898.2**	**3,043.1**	**2,839.8**
Outside UK	65.0	88.8	216.9	142.7	139.9	185.2	184.8
Total identifiable expenditure	**2,599.8**	**2,808.3**	**3,535.0**	**2,974.9**	**3,038.1**	**3,228.3**	**3,024.6**
Non-identifiable expenditure	2,284.0	2,661.0	2,531.0	2,647.0	2,677.0	2,822.0	2,864.5
Total expenditure on services	**4,883.8**	**5,469.3**	**6,066.0**	**5,621.9**	**5,715.1**	**6,050.3**	**5,889.1**

Notes:

The data presented in this table are consistent with the Country and Regional Analyses (CRA) published by HM Treasury in Chapter 9 of Public Expenditure Statistical Analyses (PESA) 2007. The figures were taken from the HM Treasury public spending database in December 2006 and the regional distributions were completed in January and February 2007. **Therefore the tables may not show the latest position and are not consistent with other tables in the Departmental Report.**

The analyses are set within the overall framework of Total Expenditure on Services (TES). TES broadly represents the current and capital expenditure of the public sector, with some differences from the national accounts measure Total Managed Expenditure. The tables show the central government and public corporation elements of TES. They include current and capital spending by the Department and its NDPBs, and public corporations' capital expenditure, but do not include capital finance to public corporations. They do not include payments to local authorities or local authorities' own expenditure. TES is a near-cash measure of public spending. The tables do not include depreciation, cost of capital charges, or movements in provisions that are in Departmental budgets. They do include pay, procurement, capital expenditure, and grants and subsidies to individuals and private sector enterprises.

Departmental spend, which is allocated on a regional basis, includes the grant to the Welsh Fourth Channel Authority, funding of eight regional Cultural Consortia, and grant to the Greater London Authority. Some NDPBs sponsored by the Department also allocated funding on a regional basis. For example, the Museums, Libraries and Archives Council allocates funding to support regional museums and Arts Council England provides support to a portfolio of regularly funded regional organisations.

The data are based on a subset of spending – identifiable expenditure on services – which is capable of being analysed as being for the benefit of individual countries and regions. Expenditure that is incurred for the benefit of the UK as a whole is excluded. Tourism allocation has been reclassified from non-identifiable to identifiable expenditure.

Across Government, most expenditure is not planned or allocated on a regional basis. Social security payments, for example, are paid to eligible individuals irrespective of where they live. Expenditure on other programmes is allocated by looking at how all the projects across the Department's area of responsibility, usually England, compare. So the analyses show the regional outcome of spending decisions that on the whole have not been made primarily on a regional basis.

Department for Culture, Media and Sport
Total spending per head by country and region

£ Million	2001-02 Outturn	2002-03 Outturn	2003-04 Outturn	2004-05 Outturn	2005-06 Outturn	2006-07 Plans	2007-08 Plans
North East	65.9	53.0	70.6	60.9	55.3	51.5	46.3
North West	36.0	39.8	42.9	38.9	41.6	32.9	30.4
Yorkshire and Humberside	47.8	46.3	54.1	40.4	46.4	46.2	42.6
East Midlands	39.3	42.4	45.5	47.8	35.5	40.9	38.1
West Midlands	34.6	38.1	63.3	35.4	40.0	43.5	40.6
Eastern	34.1	30.7	35.7	32.9	31.6	33.5	31.0
London	63.4	76.1	108.9	68.5	86.4	98.6	94.1
South East	32.1	35.3	40.2	37.7	33.3	36.5	34.2
South West	36.0	44.2	52.2	59.6	42.5	55.2	49.9
Total England	**42.1**	**45.3**	**57.3**	**46.2**	**46.4**	**49.7**	**46.4**
Scotland	38.8	39.9	35.9	43.1	46.8	35.3	31.2
Wales	65.4	68.0	70.0	80.1	75.3	82.0	76.6
Northern Ireland	39.9	41.9	42.7	37.1	55.6	56.7	50.3
Total UK identifiable expenditure	**42.9**	**45.8**	**55.7**	**47.3**	**48.1**	**50.3**	**46.7**

Notes:

The data presented in this table are consistent with the Country and Regional Analyses (CRA) published by HM Treasury in Chapter 9 of Public Expenditure Statistical Analyses (PESA) 2007. The figures were taken from the HM Treasury public spending database in December 2006 and the regional distributions were completed in January and February 2007. Therefore the tables may not show the latest position and are not consistent with other tables in the Departmental Report.

Please see additional notes on page 68.

Department for Culture, Media and Sport
Spending by function or programme by country and region 2005-06

	North East	North West	Yorkshire & Humberside	East Midlands	West Midlands	Eastern	London	South East	South West
International services									
International development assistance	1.9	0.8	4.8	0.5	1.7	0.4	0.2	0.3	0.4
Total: international services	1.9	0.8	4.8	0.5	1.7	0.4	0.2	0.3	0.4
Enterprise and economic development									
Support for business	0.9	2.5	1.3	1.2	2.4	2.5	24.6	5.4	2.8
Total: enterprise and economic development	0.9	2.5	1.3	1.2	2.4	2.5	24.6	5.4	2.8
Recreation, culture and religion									
Broadcasting	0.1	0.1	0.1	0.1	0.1	0.1	0.3	0.1	0.1
Heritage, arts, libraries and films	58.3	81.2	76.5	64.6	81.0	72.0	249.2	116.6	80.6
Lottery	70.6	181.7	137.5	72.1	110.8	88.4	325.4	130.2	118.5
Other recreation, culture and religion	2.6	5.0	4.2	2.7	3.8	3.2	10.9	4.8	3.9
Sport and recreation	7.2	13.7	10.5	11.4	14.7	8.7	39.3	14.6	9.2
Total: recreation, culture and religion	138.7	281.8	228.7	151.0	210.3	172.3	625.1	266.3	212.2
Social protection									
Public sector occupational pensions	0.0	0.0	0.0	0.0	0.0	0.0	0.0	0.0	0.0
Total: social protection	0.0	0.0	0.0	0.0	0.0	0.0	0.0	0.0	0.0
TOTAL	141.5	285.1	234.8	152.7	214.4	175.5	649.9	272.0	215.4

England	Scotland	Wales	Northern Ireland	UK identifiable expenditure	Outside UK	Total identifiable expenditure	Non-identifiable	£ Millions totals
11.0	0.0	0.0	0.0	11.0	0.0	11.0	0.0	11.0
11.0	0.0	0.0	0.0	11.0	0.0	11.0	0.0	11.0
43.6	3.4	1.1	0.4	48.5	0.5	49.0	0.0	49.0
43.6	3.4	1.1	0.4	48.5	0.5	49.0	0.0	49.0
1.0	0.1	92.3	0.1	93.5	0.0	93.5	2,677.0	2,770.5
880.0	11.2	12.4	5.1	908.7	136.0	1,044.7	0.0	1,044.7
1,235.1	218.3	112.4	88.6	1,654.5	0.0	1,654.5	0.0	1,654.5
40.9	4.2	3.9	1.7	50.7	2.5	53.2	0.0	53.2
129.3	1.5	0.5	0.0	131.3	0.9	132.2	0.0	132.2
2,286.3	235.3	221.6	95.5	2,838.7	139.4	2,978.1	2,677.0	5,655.1
0.0	0.0	0.0	0.0	0.0	0.0	0.0	0.0	0.0
0.0	0.0	0.0	0.0	0.0	0.0	0.0	0.0	0.0
2,340.9	238.7	222.7	95.9	2,898.2	139.9	3,038.1	2,677.0	5,715.1

Notes:

The data presented in this table are consistent with the Country and Regional Analyses (CRA) published by HM Treasury in Chapter 9 of Public Expenditure Statistical Analyses (PESA) 2007. The figures were taken from the HM Treasury public spending database in December 2006 and the regional distributions were completed in January and February 2007. **Therefore the tables may not show the latest position and are not consistent with other tables in the Departmental Report.**

The functional analyses are based on the United Nations Classification of the Functions of Government (COFOG), the international standard. The presentations of spending by function are consistent with those used in Chapter 9 of PESA 2007. These are not the same as the strategic priorities shown elsewhere in the report.

It is not possible to forecast drawdown from the National Lottery Distribution Fund (NLDF) with absolute accuracy because, for a variety of reasons, successful applicants draw down Lottery grants at a different rate than expected by distributing bodies. From 2002-03 to 2004-05, drawdown from the NLDF was respectively £0.4 billion, £.03 billion and £0.1 billion lower than forecast. In 2005-06, drawdown was about £70 million higher than expected and in 2006-07, less than £40 million lower than forecast. These consistently smaller discrepancies show that the Department is learning to anticipate drawdown patterns in the estimates, based on drawdown forecasts from distributors, which it puts forward.

Notes

Notes on Resource and Capital Budgets

1. The following notes relate to the Departmental Expenditure Limit (DEL) and Annually Managed Expenditure (AME) tables on pages 60 – 63.

2. The table on page 60 focuses on resource DEL. It shows that, between 2001-02 and 2007-08, resource DEL will have risen by 33% in real terms, an expected average annual real growth of 5.5%.

3. Looking at sectoral figures in this table:

   ■ growth in the spending of museums and galleries in part reflects additional funds to compensate for free access, the first full year of which was 2002-03;

   ■ figures for Libraries (mainly the British Library) and the Museums, Libraries and Archives Council (MLA) are affected by a re-classification in 2006-07 of certain grants from resource to capital. While the department clarifies the extent to which these grants should be resource or capital, resource and capital figures should be looked at together. In particular, the growth in total spending by the MLA in recent years reflects the increase in spending on *Renaissance in the Regions*, which began in 2002 and is planned to grow to a maximum of £45 million in 2007-08;

   ■ spending on the arts will have grown by 41% in real terms between 2001-02 and 2007-08, an average annual real terms growth of 7%. Allowing for spending on Creative Partnerships of £36 million in 2007-08, average annual growth on all other arts spending is 5%;

   ■ growth in spending on sport and recreation is explained by the investment in the Elite Athletes scheme during the run up to London 2012 comprising £18.8 million in 2006-07 and £29.7 million in 2007-08. The one-off spending in 2002-03 represents additional expenditure relating to the Commonwealth Games;

   ■ spending on the Royal Parks Agency peaked in 2001-02 when a revaluation in their residential estate led to a large impairment charge of £18 million. The lower figures for 2006-07 and 2007-08 are the result of a transfer to the Home Office for the policing of the Royal Parks;

   ■ spending on tourism peaked in 2002-03 because additional funds were made available in that year to mitigate the impact of foot and mouth disease on tourism; and from 1 April 2003 the English Tourist Board and the British Tourist Authority were merged into VisitBritain; and

   ■ broadcasting and media comprises funding for S4C, which is indexed to the retail prices index; and the UK Film Council.

4. Turning to annually managed expenditure (AME) on resource (page 61):

- the large figures for museums, galleries and libraries and architecture and the historic environment in 2003-04 represents an adjustment for pension purposes. The increase is due to the cost of transferring certain NDPBs pensions into the Principal Civil Service Pension Scheme from their by analogy schemes.

- the figures for broadcasting and media are solely disbursements of the BBC Licence Fee; and

- National Lottery sums available to distributors comprise both resource and capital. Lottery distributors spend the income in response to external applications and may support projects which are either capital or revenue, or a mixture of both. The capital/resource split of expenditure by distributors varies between individual distributors depending on the nature of their businesses and the widely differing sectors they support.

5. Figures for the Department's capital DEL are affected by the re-classification of certain grants from resource to capital. That aside, the notable features in the table on page 62 include:

- the step increase in sports spending in 2006-07 is a result of the setting up of the Football Foundation and the National Sports Foundation;

- spending on the Olympics has risen sharply and been funded by transfers from the Department for Communities and Local Government;

- under administration and research, the Department's refurbishment of 2-4 Cockspur Street. This moves nearly all staff into open plan and enables the release of accommodation in three other buildings. Further savings will be delivered from 2007-08 onwards from security, messengerial and facilities management and energy reductions delivered as a result of operating only two buildings; and

- the increase in expenditure in relation to the gambling and gaming board are associated with the costs of setting up the Gambling Commission.

6. On the capital budget within annually managed expenditure (page 63):

- the museum and galleries data relate to the value of art works accepted by HM Revenue and Customs in lieu of inheritance tax; and

- broadcasting and media figures show the capital consumption of resources by the BBC.

Index

Enquiries

If you have any enquiries about the work or services of the Department please contact General Enquiries on 020 7211 6200 or email enquiries@culture.gov.uk

You can also email Ministers directly:

Secretary of State
Rt Hon Tessa Jowell MP
tessa.jowell@culture.gov.uk

Minister for Culture
David Lammy MP
david.lammy@culture.gov.uk

Minister for Sport
Rt Hon Richard Caborn MP
richard.caborn@culture.gov.uk

Minister for Creative Industries and Tourism
Shaun Woodward MP
shaun.woodward@culture.gov.uk

Acknowledgements

DCMS would like to thank all the members of the public who volunteered their time to take part in the photoshoots.

Thanks also to the organisations involved including:

Angela and Georgina from Birmingham Royal Ballet

Jake from Brighton and Hove City Libraries

Sophie from Britten Sinfonia

Mike from Broad Street BID

James from GB Wheelchair Rugby Association

David from Leaps and Bounds

Becca from LSO Discovery

Gareth and the LSO St Luke's Community Choir

Nina and Victoria from mima

Karen, Emily and Jean-Pierre from Oxford Castle

Jason and Melinda from the Royal Parks Agency

Cara from RNIB Volunteer Development

Caroline and Claire from Sheffield Galleries and Museums Trust

James from Talented Athlete Scholarship Scheme

Design: red-stone.com

Photography: Nick David

except page 10 top: Olympic Delivery Authority

page 10 bottom: London 2012

page 14 top: Red Stone design

page 14 bottom: © Queen's Printer and Controller of HMSO, 2007. UK Government Art Collection

page 18: Red Stone design

page 22 top: Youth Sport Trust

page 22 bottom: Sport England

page 26 top: Visit Britain

page 30 top: Michael Cross © Café Gallery Projects London

page 30 bottom: Encounters Short Film Festival

Copies of this publication can be provided in alternative formats. For further information please contact the DCMS Publicity Unit: publications@culture.gsi.gov.uk

Printed on Revive Silk made from 75% de-inked post-consumer waste.

Printed in the UK for The Stationery Office on behalf of the Controller of Her Majesty's Stationery Office.

ID5551088 05/07